WHO ——— WAS — WHO
IN – AND – AROUND
THE ——— SECRET
ANNEXE ———— ?

anne frank house

THE PEOPLE IN HIDING

——— **HERMANN VAN PELS** ———

'...the joke-teller, something of a pessimist, always smoking, and somewhat restless.'

Miep Gies, 1996[5]

——— **AUGUSTE VAN PELS** ———

'...she was very chic and elegant'.

Bertel Freund-Hess, cousin of Hermann van Pels, 1997[6]

——— **PETER VAN PELS** ———

'A quiet boy.'

Eva Meyer, a close friend of Otto Frank's, 2010[7]

——— **FRITZ PFEFFER** ———

'In the first place my father was a sportsman, he loved to row, loved to ride horses, he liked to climb mountains.'

Werner Pfeffer, 1995[8]

THE PEOPLE IN HIDING

THE HELPERS

P. 145 —— JAN GIES ——

'Friendly, but very reserved.'

Eva Geiringer-Schloss,
Otto Frank's stepdaughter,
2008[13]

P. 153 —— OTHERS IN AND AROUND 263 PRINSENGRACHT ——

'So then we came here [...], and then she [Bep]
showed off the bookcase, and she said, "Look,
my father made this, your granddad made
this," and you know, that really does
something to you.'

Cor van Wijk, Bep's son, 2007[14]

AND FURTHER

KEY TO SYMBOLS

*	in glossary	P. 168
[numeral]	sources	P. 172

Each year, more than a million visitors come to 263 Prinsengracht in Amsterdam to see The Secret Annexe with their own eyes. This is where eight Jews spent more than two years in hiding during the Second World War, helped by five people who found it perfectly natural to assume such a dangerous responsibility.

As they make their way through the Annexe, many visitors ask themselves how it must have felt to live in hiding for two years. What was daily life like for these people? What did they eat, and indeed what did they do all day long? How did the helpers manage to feed eight extra mouths and get their office work done without raising the suspicions of the neighbours? Who were they anyway?

The diary of the young Anne Frank has put a face on the eight occupants of the Secret Annexe and their five helpers. Before going into hiding Anne was only vaguely aware of their existence, but between July 1942 and August 1944 she spent two intensive years with them. The portraits she painted in her diary were strongly coloured by both her youthful outlook and the brutal circumstances of the war years.

This book is a fresh introduction to the 13 people whom Anne's diary has rendered unforgettable: the people in hiding – Otto, Edith, Margot and Anne Frank, Hermann, Auguste and Peter van Pels and Fritz Pfeffer, and the helpers Johannes Kleiman, Victor Kugler, Bep Voskuijl and Miep and Jan Gies. It describes their lives before, during and after the hiding period. Besides the helpers there were others who were also part of the life in and around 263 Prinsengracht: people who were important to those in hiding because they provided such things as food, but also people who had to be kept in the dark, such as the warehouse workers, delivery men and sales representatives. Their roles are described here as well.

For years, the Anne Frank House has been conducting research on all those involved. This book takes the most recent insights into account, which we hope will answer many of the questions asked by visitors and readers alike.

Ronald Leopold
Executive Director, Anne Frank House

263 Prinsengracht is a typical 17th-century Amsterdam canalside house: a tall, deep structure with many rooms both large and small, steep stairways and narrow corridors. It consists of a front and a back section (*voorhuis* and *achterhuis** in Dutch architectural terminology; see cross section of the building, pp. 8-9). The building has been renovated and modified several times over the years. In the three centuries of its existence it has gone from private residence to commercial premises, and from hiding place to museum.

The Secret Annexe*, which was part of Otto Frank's office building, has become world famous because of Anne's diary. Otto Frank was the only one of the eight occupants of the Secret Annexe to survive the Holocaust*. After the eight were arrested on 4 August 1944, the Annexe was cleared out by the Puls removal company* by order of the German occupiers. In June 1945, Otto Frank found the rooms empty and abandoned. For him, that emptiness symbolized the loss of his fellow sufferers who had not returned from the camps. For this reason he later decided that the house should remain empty. And that is how museum visitor sees the Secret Annexe today: empty, except for a few authentic elements.

Cross section of the building at 263 Prinsengracht

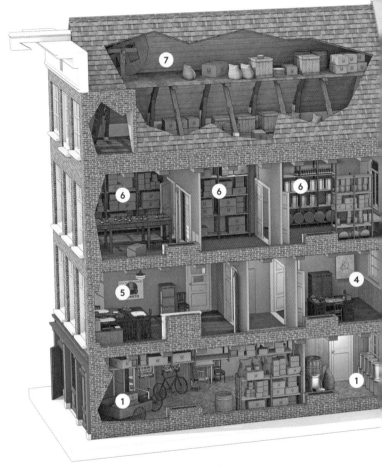

FRONT HOUSE

1 — Warehouse

2 — Company kitchen

3 — Door to Otto Frank's private office

4 — Victor Kugler's office

5 — Office of Johannes Kleiman, Miep Gies and Bep Voskuijl

6 — Storage area

7 — Attic

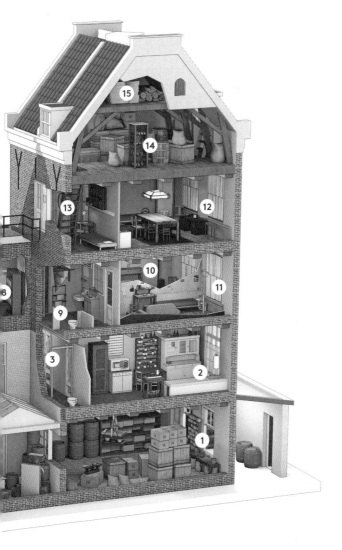

BACK HOUSE (ANNEXE)

8 — Landing with the revolving bookcase leading to the Secret Annexe

9 — Washroom

10 — Otto, Edith and Margot Frank's room

11 — Room that Anne Frank shared with Fritz Pfeffer

12 — Common living and dining room, at night the bedroom of Hermann and Auguste van Pels

13 — Peter van Pels's room

14 — Attic

15 — Loft

A BRIEF HISTORY

Germany's defeat in the First World War in 1918 brought the country to its knees. It wasn't only the heavy war reparations* that dealt such a crushing blow. The political opponents of the young Weimar Republic* also posed a great threat: the conservatives, the Communists and the National Socialists, among them Adolf Hitler. The hyperinflation* of 1923 marked the low point in Germany's crisis. The United States responded by offering loans that were intended to help pay off the war debt, enabling Germany to enjoy relative prosperity and moderate political stability until 1929. In that year, however, a worldwide economic crisis struck, causing Germany's problems to take a sharp turn for the worse. The American loans were withdrawn, many companies went bankrupt and unemployment spiralled. This produced a climate in which the extreme nationalistic ideas of Hitler and the Nazionalsozialistische Deutsche Arbeiterpartei (NSDAP, or the Nazi Party) found fertile soil. The Nazis blamed all the political and economic problems on the Jews.

After the appointment of Hitler as chancellor on 30 January 1933 and the subsequent victory of the National Socialists in the parliamentary and municipal elections, the curtain fell on the Weimar Republic. The persecution of Hitler's political opponents had already been set in motion. As the years passed, the situation became increasingly threatening for the Jews as well. Countless regulations and ordinances turned them into second-class citizens. Jews were not allowed to practise certain professions, for example. Their children had to attend separate schools and the publication of Jewish newspapers and magazines was declared illegal. Disabled people were also persecuted, as were Roma* and Sinti*, homosexuals and Jehovah's Witnesses*. Later on, most of these regulations were also imposed in countries occupied by Germany – and that included the Netherlands.

Voor Joden verboden

DE PROCUREUR-GENERAAL
FUNG. GEWESTELIJK DIRECTEUR VAN POLITIE

VAN GENECHTEN

IN SEPTEMBER 1941
SIGNS LIKE THIS
ONE, 'PROHIBITED
FOR JEWS' BEGAN
APPEARING IN PARKS,
CAFÉS, RESTAURANTS
AND THEATRES.

On the run
—

After Hitler came to power, a large number of German Jews fled their homeland. Tens of thousands went to the Netherlands. Among them were Otto and Edith Frank and their daughters Margot and Anne, and Hermann and Auguste van Pels and their son Peter. The eighth occupant of the Secret Annexe*, Fritz Pfeffer, first tried to emigrate from Germany to South America, but in the end he too ended up in the Netherlands.

For some refugees the Netherlands was meant to be a stopover point in the search for a safe refuge. The Frank and Van Pels families also attempted to leave the country. In 1937 Otto Frank tried to set up a business in England, but his efforts failed. In 1938 he applied for emigration to the United States but was turned down. After Edith's unmarried brothers did succeed in getting to America, Otto made a few more frantic attempts to emigrate to America or Cuba in 1941. But due to the growing stream of refugees, the excessive red tape and the ever-changing demands, all these requests came to naught. The Van Pels family had been on a waiting list to apply for a visa to the United States since 1939, and Fritz Pfeffer was hoping to go to Australia, Aruba or Chile.

When all these attempts failed, they literally had nowhere left to go. Finally, just over two years after the German invasion of the Netherlands, they decided to go into hiding.

The occupation and the anti-Jewish regulations
—

On 10 May 1940, Nazi Germany invaded the Netherlands. After a four-day battle and the devastating bombing of Rotterdam, the country capitulated. The Dutch government and Queen Wilhelmina fled to London, from which they made radio broadcasts via Radio Oranje on the BBC to raise the spirits of their countrymen. Listening had to be done in secret because the German occupiers had banned the English stations, and it wasn't long before the Dutch were required to turn in their radios as well.

The Nazis also introduced more and more anti-Jewish regulation in the Netherlands. The names of approximately 140,000 Jews were entered in a central Jewish registry; they all had to wear a Jewish star* on their clothing; they had to turn in their bicycles; they could no longer travel by tram, could no longer attend the theatre or cinema, could not be out on the street or sit in their own gardens between eight in the evening and six in the morning, could not marry Gentiles and could not participate in public sports. Jewish children had to go to Jewish schools. In short, regulations that made it impossible to live a normal life.

But the Nazis would go much further. At the Wannsee Conference* of January 1942, high-ranking Nazi officials discussed the strategy for the *Endlösung**. In July of that year the systematic deportation of Jews was set in motion. The implementation of the Nazi plans for the deportation and extermination of millions of European Jews had begun.

Opekta, Pectacon, Gies & Co
—

The Franks, a young Frankfurt family of prominent social standing, come to the Netherlands in 1933 because Otto Frank is able to set up a business there. The business in question is Opekta, which Otto has learned about from his brother-in-law, Erich Elias, who works for the company in Basel. Opekta manufactures and sells pectin, a gelatinous substance used to make jam, and Otto's job is to corner the Dutch retail market. He rents commercial space on the Nieuwezijds Voorburgwal and hires an office staff that includes Victor Kugler and Miep Santrouschitz, as well as a couple of warehouse workers. In 1937 he takes on Bep Voskuijl as secretary; later Bep's father, Johannes Voskuijl, will join the firm as warehouse supervisor.

WIJ VERHUIZEN!

Vanaf 1 December 1940 zijn onze kantoren en magazijnen verplaatst van Singel 400 naar **Prinsengracht 263** bij den Westertoren Telefoonnummers blijven ongewijzigd.

HANDELSMAATSCHAPPIJ **PECTACON** N.V.
Specerijen en Conserveermiddelen
AMSTERDAM-C.
Prinsengracht 263   Telefoon 35293-37059.

PECTACON CHANGE-OF-ADDRESS NOTICE.

PECTACON STAMP FOR BOUILLON EXTRACT.

The sale of pectin gradually increases, but because it's a seasonal product – there's less fresh fruit available in the winter, and certainly during those years – Otto Frank searches for a way to expand his operations. In 1938 he launches Pectacon, a company that mixes and sells spices and other ingredients used in the production of foodstuffs. Joining him in this venture is Johannes Kleiman, whom he has known for several years. Otto also hires a spice specialist, Hermann van Pels, who has recently fled from Germany with his family. From 400 Singel, where both companies are now located, they begin looking for a commercial space that can accommodate grinding machines on the ground floor and that is also more accessible for delivery men.

On 1 December 1940 they move into a large building at 263 Prinsengracht, which is divided into a front section, or *voorhuis*, and a back section, or *achterhuis**. The ground floor, which runs all the way back beneath the *achterhuis*, is used as a warehouse and work area. Located here are the packing tables, the spice mill and the grinding machines. On the first floor, in both the *voorhuis* and the *achterhuis*, are the offices and a kitchen; the second floor of the voorhuis serves as storage space. The two upper floors of the *achterhuis*, including the attic and loft, are empty (for a cross section of the building see pp. 8-9).

THE LOGO OF GIES &
CO FEATURING THE
WESTERTOREN:
A REFERENCE TO
THE COMPANY'S
LOCATION, 1941.

14

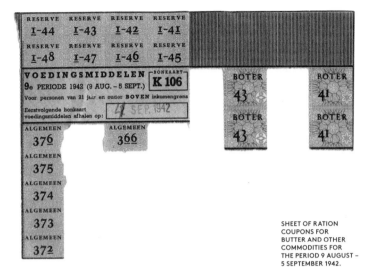

RESERVE RESERVE RESERVE RESERVE
I-44 I-43 I-42 I-41
RESERVE RESERVE RESERVE RESERVE
I-48 I-47 I-46 I-45

VOEDINGSMIDDELEN ┌─BONKAART─┐ K 106
9e PERIODE 1942 (9 AUG. – 5 SEPT.)
Voor personen van 21 jaar en ouder BOVEN inkomengrens
Eerstvolgende bonkaart
voedingsmiddelen afhalen op: 4 SEP. 1942

BOTER 43   BOTER 41
BOTER 43   BOTER 41

ALGEMEEN   ALGEMEEN
37<u>6</u>   3<u>66</u>
ALGEMEEN
375
ALGEMEEN
374
ALGEMEEN
373
ALGEMEEN
37<u>2</u>

SHEET OF RATION
COUPONS FOR
BUTTER AND OTHER
COMMODITIES FOR
THE PERIOD 9 AUGUST –
5 SEPTEMBER 1942.

In late 1941, when an ordinance comes into effect prohibiting Jews from running businesses, Otto, Kleiman, Kugler and Miep's husband, Jan Gies, devise a construction to hoodwink the occupiers. Kleiman becomes the director of Opekta, and Pectacon's operations are continued under the guise of a new firm, Gies & Co, with Victor Kugler as manager and Jan Gies as supervising director. To the outside world, both of Otto Frank's companies have now become Aryanized*.

The hiding period and the arrest
—

In the early spring of 1942, with the situation for Jews in the Netherlands becoming increasingly forbidding, Otto Frank, with the help of Kugler, Kleiman and Van Pels, begins work in the Secret Annexe to turn it into a hiding place for the Frank and Van Pels families. This was quite unusual: most families split up to reduce the chance of discovery. Otto asks his office staff if they are prepared to help the families when the time comes. All of them agree without hesitation, even Bep Voskuijl, who is only 22 years old.

They choose 13 July as the date to go into hiding. But when Margot is called up to report for a German 'work camp' on 5 July 1942, the Frank family realize they cannot wait any longer and leave for the Prinsengracht the following day. The Van Pels family follow one week later. In November of that year, Fritz Pfeffer becomes the eighth person to occupy the Annexe. For more than two years, all eight of them are confined to a space of about 120 square metres. During office hours they must keep all noise to a minimum. The irritations and tensions among them sometimes rise to fever pitch, and then there is the constant fear of being discovered.

On 4 August 1944 that fear becomes reality: they are betrayed. The eight Annexe occupants, along with Kleiman and Kugler, are taken to the headquarters of the Sicherheitsdienst* (SD), where the men are interrogated. After one night in the building of the SD and three more nights in an Amsterdam house of detention, the eight people in hiding are transported to the Westerbork transit camp on 8 August and later to the Auschwitz-Birkenau concentration camp*.

Kleiman and Kugler – declared enemies of the regime because they have come to the assistance of people in hiding – spend a few weeks in another house of detention and are then transported to Camp Amersfoort. Miep Gies and Bep Voskuijl are not arrested. In the Secret Annexe, which is in shambles after the arrest, they find Anne's writings. Miep keeps them in her desk, hoping that one day she will be able to return them to Anne.

ANNE'S DIARIES, HER BOOK OF STORIES AND BEAUTIFUL SENTENCES BOOK, AND A NUMBER OF THE LOOSE PAGES ON WHICH SHE RE-WROTE HER DIARY.

S i l b e r b a u e r   Karl
geb. 21.6.1911 in Wien
Wien 1o.,Karmaschgasse 50/51

Referat IV A 1 (Kommunismus, Marxismus)

Krim. Ass. im Ref. IV A 1
Krim. Sek.,
NSDAP seit
SS seit 28.5.1943, SS-Oberscharführer

GESTAPO REGISTRATION CARD BELONGING TO SS OBERSCHARFÜHRER KARL JOSEPH SILBERBAUER. ON 4 AUGUST 1944 HE LED THE ARREST OF THE EIGHT PEOPLE IN HIDING AND THE HELPERS KLEIMAN AND KUGLER.

Ultimately the Annexe occupants die terrible deaths in various concentration camps, the victims of deprivation, inhumane treatment and sickness. Except for one: Otto Frank. He comes back. The helpers also survive the war. But to a great extent the events in the Secret Annexe, the memory of their friends and the publication of Anne's diary determine the remainder of their lives.

Police investigation
—

In 1948, four years after the arrest and three years after liberation, the first police investigation of the betrayal is carried out. Various people, including the helpers and Otto Frank, are questioned as witnesses. Who might have betrayed the people in hiding? In 1963, when the identity of SD officer Karl Joseph Silberbauer is made known, there is a second attempt to find out what happened. In both investigations, Willem van Maaren, the warehouse supervisor, is one of the suspects. But although it is clear that Van Maaren committed several robberies in the Prinsengracht building, it cannot be proven that he is the guilty party. Despite other theories, new investigations and a number of possible suspects, the identity of the person who betrayed the occupants of the Secret Annexe has never been established.

The helpers are honoured

In 1971, Johannes Kleiman, Victor Kugler, Bep Voskuijl and Miep and Jan Gies, through the intervention of Otto Frank, each receive a Yad Vashem award, that of 'Righteous Among the Nations'. This award is presented to Gentiles who helped Jews go into hiding, escape or survive during the Second World War. The helpers are given medals, and trees are planted in their honour in the Avenue of the Righteous on the Mount of Remembrance in Jerusalem.

VICTOR KUGLER'S YAD VASHEM AWARD. ALONG THE LOWER EDGE, IN FRENCH, ARE THE WORDS, 'HE WHO SAVES ONE LIFE SAVES A WHOLE UNIVERSE'.

DAILY LIFE IN
THE SECRET ANNEXE

Daily routine
—

It's a quarter to seven. The alarm clock goes off in the Secret Annexe*. The eight occupants get up and get washed before the warehouse workers arrive at half past eight. After that they must keep all noise to a minimum. They walk in slippers, avoid the creaking stairs and don't use any running water. Coughing, sneezing, laughing, talking or quarrelling is absolutely forbidden. To kill time, the eight mainly spend the morning reading and studying. Some do needlework, others prepare the next meal. In the office on the first floor the helpers are at work. Miep takes time to pick up the shopping list from the Secret Annexe.

'It's twelve-thirty. The whole gang breathes a sigh of relief'[15], Anne writes. At noontime the warehouse workers go home to eat and the Annexe occupants can relax a little. The helpers from the office usually drop in, and Jan Gies sometimes joins them. At one o'clock they all listen to the BBC on the illegal 'little baby radio'[16], followed by lunch. After the lunch break the helpers go back downstairs and most of the occupants take naps. Anne often uses this time to write in her diary. Silence prevails for the rest of the afternoon: potatoes are peeled, quiet chores are done for the office and the reading and studying continue. The helpers go on with their office work. Miep and Bep slip out during the afternoon or after office hours to work their way through the shopping list: food, clothing, soap and sometimes birthday presents.

When the warehouse workers leave at around half past five, Bep gives the occupants a sign. Each of the helpers returns to his or her own spouse or family and the Secret Annexe comes to life: someone grabs the warehouse key and fetches the bread, typewriters are carried upstairs, potatoes are set to boil, the cat door in the coal store is opened for Peter's cat Mouschi. Each has his or her own task. After dinner they sometimes play a game. At around nine o'clock the occupants get their sleeping arrangements ready, with much shuffling of chairs and foldaway beds. They take turns going to the bathroom. Anne, being the youngest, goes first. Fritz stays up late studying Spanish in the office downstairs. By about midnight the whole Secret Annexe is fast asleep.

On Saturday morning the warehouse workers put in half a day's work, but on Saturday afternoon and Sunday the Annexe occupants take time for a full sponge bath in a basin, each in his own favourite spot in the building. The laundry is done then too, and the Secret Annexe is cleaned. There are businesses located in the two adjacent buildings, so when the weekends come the occupants don't have to be quite so cautious. But the curtains must always remain closed.

Food and distribution

—

Before going into hiding, the Annexe occupants stocked up on a great many supplies including rice, jam, flour, tea, coffee and about a hundred tins of food, as well as soap and other household products. After a few months 130 kilos of dried legumes are added to the store. As Peter is heaving each of the heavy bags up to the attic, one of them suddenly splits open and a torrent of brown beans comes cascading down the stairs. It takes weeks before the last beans are found: they're in every hook and cranny of the stairwell.

Because of the threat of food shortages, the Dutch government began to regulate the food supply even before the Nazi invasion by means of ration registration cards* and ration coupons*. The occupiers decided to continue using this system. Everyone listed in the municipal register was required to appear in person at their town hall to pick up a registration card. They could then go to a rationing office (or have someone else go for them), where ration coupons could be obtained on presentation of this card. By showing the registration cards of the Franks and Pfeffer, Miep and Bep are able to obtain ration coupons to buy certain provisions and other rationed products, such as soap. But because the Van Pels family have not been listed in the municipal register since December 1942, they have no registration card and therefore no coupons. They have to buy everything on the black market, which is much more expensive. The two families maintain separate household account books: they do eat together, but after a while they divide up the oil ration, for example, and count out the potatoes per person.

Sometimes there's nothing to be had but endive, spinach or sauerkraut, and the Annexe occupants eat the same thing for weeks on end. For a while potatoes constitute the basis of almost every meal, even breakfast when there's no bread. In May 1944, Anne writes with her typical sense of humour: 'Vegetables are still very

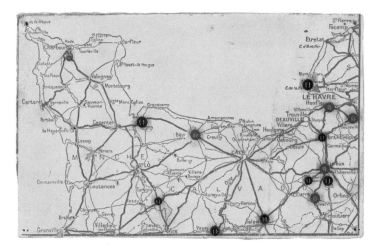

THE SECRET ANNEXE OCCUPANTS ARE OVERJOYED TO HEAR OF THE ALLIED FORCES LANDING IN

NORMANDY ON 6 JUNE 1944. OTTO CHARTS THEIR PROGRESS WITH PINS ON A MAP.

hard to come by. This afternoon we had rotten boiled lettuce. [...] Add to that rotten potatoes, and you have a meal fit for a king!'[17]

Contact with the outside world
—

Cut off from the world as they are, the people in hiding attach great importance to all incoming news. So whenever the helpers come to visit, they hang on their every word. Kugler frequently shows up with newspapers and weeklies such as the *Haagsche Post** and *Das Reich**. Every scrap of information is turned inside out and discussed over and over again. After only five months, Anne writes: 'Our thoughts are subject to as little change as we are'.[18]

Through Miep, Fritz Pfeffer corresponds regularly with his beloved Charlotte. He also receives letters and treats from her.

The penetrating peal of the Westertoren bells, only a few dozen metres away, rings out every 15 minutes. At night the Annexe occupants often hear the terrifying sound of bombers flying overhead. Tuning in to the illegal radio, they listen to Radio Oranje on the BBC and to the German stations. The tension they feel as they listen is intense, especially after D-Day* in 1944 when reports come in of the advance of the Allied troops. At this point Otto begins marking their progress on a map.

Daily discomforts

The Secret Annexe* is damp and out of alignment in places. Most of the windows have to be kept closed to avoid discovery, which makes it oppressive and stuffy inside. On weekdays the toilet cannot be flushed during office hours, and on top of that many of the occupants smoke. A pungent odour hangs in the air of the Secret Annexe, mixed with that of pepper and nutmeg. When a large amount of pepper is being ground downstairs, Anne writes: 'Everyone who comes upstairs greets us with an "ah-CHOO".'[19] Rats and mice are unavoidable in an old canalside house filled with supplies. The cats Boche and Mouschi are on the prowl every night, but at one point they themselves cause an infestation of fleas: everyone starts itching!

One of the group's main fears is that someone might become seriously ill. Fortunately, their maladies are limited to headaches, bad colds (no coughing or sneezing during the daytime!), flu, Anne's deteriorating eyesight, Auguste's bruised rib and decayed molar and Otto's backache.

To keep fit the group do gymnastics during the first year. They also practise great mental discipline to endure the confinement and silence.

Holidays

No birthday is ever passed over in the Secret Annexe, including those of the helpers. Because food and interesting presents are increasingly difficult to come by, the occupants become more and more inventive. Auguste is given a cheese, meat and bread coupon and a pot of jam, for instance, and Peter receives a stock market game. Mostly they give each other books, food or flowers, and the Frank family write each other poems. In January 1944 Edith is given a 'real mocha cake, pre-war quality'[20], which Anne's father specifically asks her to mention in her diary. Towards the end of the hiding period, even a rather well-preserved 'serving of coffee'[21] is given as a present. For Christmas 1943 Miep bakes a cake with 'Peace 1944' written on top, and for Sinterklaas* everyone gets his or her own shoe as a joke, accompanied by a poem.

OTTO FRANK

1936

NAME	————————————	OTTO HEINRICH FRANK
BORN	————————————	12 MAY 1889
		(FRANKFURT AM MAIN, GERMANY)
DIED	————————————	19 AUGUST 1980
		(BASEL, SWITZERLAND)

Miep Gies, 1996[22] ———————————— 'Mr Frank was the calm one, the children's teacher, the most logical, the one who balanced everyone out. He was the leader, the one in charge. When a decision had to be made, all eyes turned to Mr Frank.'

OTTO FRANK

Otto Frank is the second son of Michael Frank and Alice Betty Stern. He has an older brother and a younger brother and sister. His family owns the Bankhaus Michael Frank in Frankfurt, which specializes in stockbroking, bill broking and exchange trading. The Jewish Frank family is well-to-do. From the age of twelve, Otto lives in a stately villa on Beethovenplatz. After gymnasium he studies art history for one semester and then goes to work in a bank. Between 1909 and 1911 Otto works in New York, first as a sales assistant at Macy's department store and then, once again, at a bank. When his father unexpectedly dies in September 1909 he returns home for a brief visit.

After going back to Germany for good, Otto works for various firms until he is called up for the army in 1915, for Germany is at war. He is appointed telephone switchboard operator and observer at the Western front, and in time he is promoted to lieutenant.

Because of the political and economic situation, after the First World War, the family bank finds itself in turbulent waters. Otto and his brother Herbert take over the directorship from their mother. Otto searches for new ways to earn money for the family business, and in 1923 he, his brother and his brother-in-law set up a branch of the bank in Amsterdam. This is when he meets Johannes Kleiman, whom he appoints assignee with power of attorney*. In 1927 Otto also takes charge of the Sodener Mineralprodukte company, which makes mineral pastilles and has long been in family hands. He works for the family bank until 1932, when it finally goes bankrupt.

In 1925, at the age of 36, Otto marries Edith Holländer. They have two daughters, Margot and Anne. Otto enjoys reading, which he does in his rare free time. He always makes time for his children: they play games together, he takes lots of pictures of them and patiently answers all their questions. He takes his daughters seriously and participates with Edith in their upbringing.

24

> CONTINUED ON P. 32

OTTO FRANK IN
NEW YORK, 1910.

OTTO FRANK (IN FRONT,
LEFT OF CENTRE, IN A
SAILOR SUIT) WITH HIS
FAMILY IN THE BLACK
FOREST, 1900.

OTTO FRANK
DURING THE FIRST
WORLD WAR.

OTTO FRANK

OTTO WITH
MARGOT AND ANNE,
AUGUST 1931.

OTTO AND EDITH ON
THEIR HONEYMOON
IN SAN REMO, ITALY,
MAY 1925.

OTTO, EDITH, MARGOT
AND ANNE FRANK ON
MERWEDEPLEIN IN
AMSTERDAM, MAY 1941.

OTTO FRANK (CENTRE) AFTER HIS RETURN FROM AUSCHWITZ, WITH HIS OFFICE STAFF AND HELPERS. LEFT TO RIGHT: MIEP GIES, JOHANNES KLEIMAN, VICTOR KUGLER AND BEP VOSKUIJL, 1945.

OTTO FRANK, AROUND 1970. HE RECEIVES THOUSANDS OF LETTERS DURING HIS LIFETIME FROM PEOPLE ALL OVER THE WORLD."

OTTO FRANK AND HIS
SECOND WIFE FRITZI,
WITH HER DAUGHTER
EVA AND THE
GRANDCHILDREN,
MID-SIXTIES.

> CONTINUED FROM P. 24

Otto is a considerate, outgoing and amiable man who can also be quite strict.

After Hitler assumes power in 1933, Otto and his family leave Germany and move to Merwedeplein in Amsterdam. In the years that follow, Otto and Edith regularly invite friends to their home, including Otto's employee Miep Santrouschitz and her fiancé Jan Gies, the Van Pels family and Fritz Pfeffer. Otto serves as a linchpin for many newcomers in the neighbourhood. While living on Merwedeplein he also takes time for his children; even his daughters' girlfriends later recall what a nice father he was. In the evening he likes to drink a glass of beer and on Sunday morning he sometimes brings Edith breakfast in bed.

Otto is focused on his work. In the Netherlands he sets up a branch of the German Opekta company, and later he and Kleiman launch another firm, Pectacon. He also tries to start a business in England, but this is unsuccessful. In 1941 Jews are banned from owning businesses, but by means of clever constructions he is still able to run his Dutch companies, albeit behind the scenes.

Otto Frank is the key figure in the decision to go into hiding: when his attempts at emigration don't pan out, he uses part of his office building as a hiding place. His faithful office workers agree to serve as helpers.

On 6 July 1942 the Frank family go into hiding. One week later the Van Pels family arrive, followed a little more than four months later by Fritz Pfeffer. Otto Frank is the pater familias and serves as peacekeeper when irritations threaten to get out of hand. He reads a great deal – he loves Charles Dickens – and helps Margot, Anne and Peter with their homework in the hope that after the war they'll quickly be able to re-engage at school. Otto puts the needs of others above his own. What's the first thing he'd like to do after liberation? While the others dream of a hot bath

OTTO FRANK

Flight to the Netherlands
—
Linchpin

In hiding
—
Pater familias

or a slice of cake, Otto (as Anne reports in her diary) would first like to visit the sick Johannes Voskuijl, Opekta's warehouse superintendent and father of Bep.

Otto discusses the war's progress with Van Pels, Pfeffer, Kugler and Kleiman. He also continues to play an active role in his businesses; all important decisions are submitted to him.

After discovery
—
Absorbed by the diary

On 4 August 1944, all the occupants of the Secret Annexe, along with Victor Kugler and Johannes Kleiman, are arrested and taken away. The Annexe occupants are first put in a house of detention in Amsterdam and then deported to Camp Westerbork. The conditions are poor, but they're still together. After a few weeks they're all selected for transport to the east. Upon arrival at Auschwitz-Birkenau*, the men are separated from the women. The men are put to work in Auschwitz I*, three kilometres further on. Otto will be held there for almost five months.

Otto Frank is the only one of the eight people in hiding to survive the war, having been left behind in a sick barracks when the Auschwitz concentration camp is evacuated just before its liberation by the Russians on 27 January 1945. Otto suspects that only Hermann van Pels has been killed. Peter had been forced to leave during the evacuation, and Fritz Pfeffer had already been deported. Otto knows nothing about the fate of his wife and daughters.

After liberation the difficult journey home begins. Fighting is still going on in many parts of Europe. Like thousands of others, Otto tries to obtain information about his family. On the way he learns that Edith died in Auschwitz-Birkenau after having been separated from Anne and Margot. On 3 June 1945 he arrives in Amsterdam and goes to the home of Miep and Jan Gies. He moves in with them, and after a few weeks of anxious uncertainty and endless inquiry he finally hears that Margot and Anne have also died. This is a very emotional time for Otto Frank, and, as he writes to his mother in Basel, 'I can't seem to find my balance'.[23]

Miep gives him Anne's writings, which are 'a revelation'[24] to him. He reads things about his daughter that he had never before suspected. First he translates passages for family and friends. Finally, at the urging of several acquaintances, he decides to make this intimate account public. The first edition of the book is published in 1947, and gradually it takes the whole world by storm.

In the meantime, Otto tries to keep his businesses going. He feels responsible for his employees, who did so much for him and his family. But more and more of his life is being absorbed by the diary. In 1952 Otto retires from his work – he is now 63 years old – and moves to Switzerland. All these years he has been living with Miep and Jan. One year later he marries Elfriede (Fritzi) Markovits, another Auschwitz survivor, making him the stepfather of Fritzi's daughter Eva and eventually a beloved granddad for three granddaughters. He literally stands on his head for them, even at an advanced age!

After leaving Amsterdam Otto spends most of his time working on the diary and pursuing his ideals. He devotes himself to human rights and reconciliation, and fights against right-wing radicals who deny the authenticity of the diary. With Fritzi's help he also answers thousands of letters from people all over the world. He works closely with the Anne Frank House in Amsterdam to preserve the Secret Annexe* and to organize youth conferences. Otto Frank dies on 19 August 1980 at the age of 91. People come from far and wide to pay their respects.

EDITH FRANK

1935

NAME	———————————	EDITH FRANK-HOLLÄNDER
BORN	———————————	16 JANUARY 1900
		(AACHEN, GERMANY)
DIED	———————————	6 JANUARY 1945
		(AUSCHWITZ, POLAND)

Alice Frank, ——————————— 'Edith always stood by you,
Otto's mother, through thick and thin,
1945[25] and she was a devoted
mother and best friend
for the children.'

Edith Holländer is born in Aachen, the youngest of four children in a religious Jewish family. She has two brothers and one sister. The successful family business, B. Holländer Rohprodukten-handlung, which deals in iron, scrap metal, machines, components, rags and paper, provides the family with a certain level of comfort. Edith enjoys a carefree youth, although the death of her sister Bettina in 1914 is a devastating blow. At school she is a good and diligent pupil. Edith enjoys sports: she plays tennis and swims. She likes to attend balls and big parties and loves pretty clothes. She is also very well-read.

After secondary school she works for the family business for several years. In 1925, after a brief engagement, she marries Otto Frank in the Aachen synagogue. The more than one hundred wedding guests are treated to an elegant dinner featuring salmon, roast beef and veal ragout.

After the wedding, Edith and Otto move in with his mother in Frankfurt am Main. In 1926 Margot is born. One year later the young family move to a beautiful house on Marbachweg. In 1929 Edith has another daughter, Anne. Later she writes about their time on Marbachweg: 'For us, too, the years on Marbachweg were among the best.'[26]

Because they are Jewish, their tenancy is terminated and the Frank family are forced to move to another house in Frankfurt in 1931. Shortly after this the family bank goes bankrupt. Their financial situation quickly deteriorates, making it impossible for them to pay their rent. In 1933 they move in with Otto's mother once again. After Hitler comes to power, they decide to emigrate to the Netherlands. While Otto prepares for the move, Edith looks for suitable housing in Amsterdam. In November 1933 she finds a comfortable upstairs flat on Merwedeplein. It's smaller than she's used to, but it's also 'light, practical and warm'.[27] In 1938 they begin renting out the upper floor to a series of temporary tenants.

EDITH FRANK

> CONTINUED ON P. 43

EDITH FRANK

EDITH FRANK

EDITH (SECOND
FROM THE LEFT)
ON THE BEACH
WITH HER BROTHER
WALTER (LEFT)
AND TWO FRIENDS,
AROUND 1920.

SEATED AT THE TABLE
IN THE BACK ARE
EDITH AND OTTO,
ALONG WITH EDITH'S
PARENTS AND AN AUNT,
AND A NUMBER
OF UNIDENTIFIED
GENTLEMEN. SAM REMO,
ITALY, MARCH 1925.

THE BRIDAL COUPLE:
EDITH AND OTTO
FRANK, 12 MAY 1925.

EDITH WITH MARGOT
AND THE NEWBORN
ANNE IN THEIR HOUSE
ON MARBACHWEG
IN FRANKFURT,
SUMMER 1929.

EDITH FRANK

ABOVE: EDITH, ANNE
AND MARGOT SHORTLY
BEFORE EMIGRATING
TO THE NETHERLANDS,
ON HAUPTWACHE
IN FRANKFURT,
10 MARCH 1933.

BELOW:
MERWEDEPLEIN IN
AMSTERDAM-SOUTH
IN THE THIRTIES. THE
FRANK FAMILY WILL
LIVE AT NUMBER 37.

42

> CONTINUED FROM P. 36

Edith greatly misses her old life. Now she has to do all the housework herself, whereas in Frankfurt she always had help. She also misses her family and friends, as well as German food. In March 1939 her mother, Rosa Holländer, moves in with them. When Rosa becomes ill, Edith takes care of her until her death in January 1942.

Edith often has a houseful of visitors on Saturday afternoons. She serves coffee and tea, with homemade pastries and biscuits. She learns Dutch and also takes English lessons, with a view to possibly emigrating to England or the United States. In late 1937 she writes to a girlfriend: '...I believe that all the Jews of Germany today are scouring the world and not being let in anywhere', and: 'we may be moving on further ourselves'.[28]

In hiding
—
Living in fear and despair

When Margot is called up for a 'work camp' in Germany in July 1942, the family decide to go into hiding one week earlier than planned. Edith quickly packs the last of their things. They move on Monday morning walking through the city under layers of extra clothing. Hopefully no one will notice them! Fortunately it's raining and there aren't many people outdoors. Once inside the Secret Annexe*, Edith seems apathetic and pale, according to Miep. She's is unable to move, exhausted by the tension and deeply distressed about what she's had to leave behind.

Everyone in the Secret Annexe has his or her own task in the joint housekeeping. Edith mainly does the cleaning and the washing-up. She also takes care of her family and mends their clothing. As a diversion she reads 'everything except detective stories'[29] and continues with her English course. Edith tries to raise her daughters with patience and understanding, but she frequently clashes with the precocious Anne. This is very upsetting for her. The war also weighs heavily on her mind, and she suffers from gloomy and sometimes despairing moods, which she tries to hide from the others as much as possible.

EDITH FRANK

'I saw my wife and my two daughters standing there, [...] with their hands in the air'[30], Otto Frank later attested. After the arrest, Edith and the others are first sent to Camp Westerbork. Men and women sleep and work separately but are able to spend their evenings together. During the day the women disassemble batteries, a filthy chore. After their deportation to Auschwitz-Birkenau*, the men and the women are separated for good. Edith and her daughters will never see Otto again. The conditions in the camp are barbaric: the food is meagre and poor, they stand at roll-call for hours in the rain and the cold, they are cruelly treated and the work is heavy and pointless. It's a well-organized hell.

According to witnesses, Edith and her daughters are inseparable. When Anne is sent to the sick barracks because of scabies on her arm, Margot arranges to accompany her. Edith tries to sneak bread to them. But when her daughters are selected for transport to Bergen-Belsen, she has to let them go. Edith is left alone. This compounds her suffering dramatically. Underfed and exhausted, Edith dies on 6 January 1945 in the sick barracks.

EDITH FRANK

MARGOT FRANK

1941

NAME ———————————— MARGOT BETTI FRANK
BORN ———————————— 16 FEBRUARY 1926
(FRANKFURT AM MAIN, GERMANY)
DIED ———————————— MARCH 1945
(BERGEN-BELSEN, GERMANY)

Anne Frank, ———————————— 'Margot's a stinker (there's
1942 and no other word for it)', but
1944[31] over a year later: 'Margot
[...] is becoming
a real friend.'

Margot Betti Frank is the first child of Otto Frank and Edith Frank-Holländer and a very healthy baby. When she is three years old she's joined by a sister, Anne. Margot plays with her neighbour Gertrud Naumann, who is also her babysitter, and with other children in the neighbourhood. In 1932 she starts school. Margot is a sweet and easy-going girl.

When Otto and Edith Frank decide to emigrate to the Netherlands in 1933, Margot and Anne go to stay with Granny Holländer in Aachen. They're crazy about their grandmother. Edith travels back and forth between Amsterdam and Aachen. Once the new house is in fairly good shape in late December, Edith's brothers Julius and Walter bring Margot to Amsterdam by car. Anne stays with Granny in Germany until February 1934, when she's brought to Amsterdam too and placed on the table for Margot's eighth birthday.

In the Netherlands, Margot quickly catches up with her grade level. She's a fast learner and is very conscientious, and she quickly masters the Dutch language. After primary school she goes on to the Municipal Lyceum for Girls. She is modest and always ready to help others: her girlfriends with their homework and her mother with her housework. She also helps take care of her somewhat difficult little sister. Margot gets on well with her mother. They often go together to the synagogue of the Liberal Jewish Congregation in Tolstraat.

With her big, dark eyes, olive skin and black hair, Margot grows into a pretty young lady. She dresses well and wears fashionable glasses. Margot is also athletic. In the winter she likes to skate, and she enjoys playing tennis and rowing with her classmates. In the summer of 1941, all Jewish children are ordered to attend separate schools. Margot, Anne and Margot's best friend Jetteke Frijda go to the Jewish Lyceum. The anti-Jewish climate becomes increasingly noticeable in her daily life: in June 1941 she's no longer allowed to go swimming, and in September of the same year she's banned from sports entirely.

> CONTINUED ON P. 53

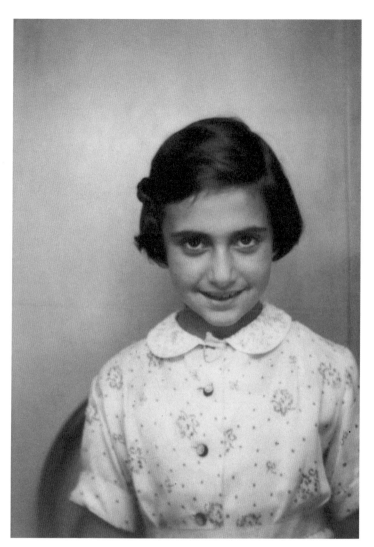

MARGOT FRANK

MARGOT FRANK

MARGOT (FAR LEFT)
PLAYING WITH THE
NEIGHBOURHOOD
CHILDREN. THE LITTLE
GIRL WITH THE LONG
BRAIDS IS GERTRUD
NAUMANN,
FRANKFURT, JULY 1929.

MARGOT WITH HER
GIRLFRIEND HETTY
LUDEL AT THE ICE
SKATING RINK,
AMSTERDAM,
WINTER 1937-1938.

MARGOT, ANNE AND
GRANNY HOLLÄNDER
ON THE BEACH,
ZANDVOORT,
JUNE 1939.

BICYCLE TRIP
ORGANIZED BY THE
MACCABI HATZAIR
ZIONIST YOUTH CLUB.
MARGOT IS AT THE FAR
LEFT, 1940 OR 1941.

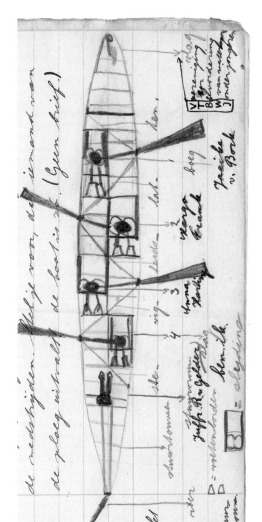

MARGOT AND HER
'DAMES 4' (4 LADIES)
WIN A MEDAL FOR
ROWING IN THE
STYLE DIVISION IN
ZAANDAM. IN 1941,
WHEN MARGOT AND
THE JEWISH COACH
ARE BANNED FROM
ROWING WITH THE
CLUB, THE WHOLE
GROUP REFUSE TO
PARTICIPATE IN
FUTURE CONTESTS.
BELLA KOHLWEY, ONE
OF MARGOT'S FELLOW
ROWERS, DREW THIS
SKETCH IN HER DIARY.
MARGOT SAT AT
POSITION 2.

MARGOT FRANK ON THE ROOF OF THE MERWEDEPLEIN HOUSE, 1940. THIS WAS PROBABLY THE 'FOLDING BED' THAT SHE SLEPT ON FOR TWO YEARS IN THE SECRET ANNEXE.[32]

> CONTINUED FROM P. 46

In May 1942 she's forced to wear the yellow Jewish star*. Yet Margot tries to lead as normal a life as possible.

In hiding
—
Eight together yet all alone

On Sunday, 5 July 1942, Margot receives a call-up to report for a German 'work camp'. This prompts the Frank family to go into hiding one week sooner than planned. Very early the next morning, and wearing many layers of clothing, Margot cycles to the Prinsengracht with Miep Gies. She has removed the yellow Jewish star* from her coat and is terribly nervous.

During the whole hiding period Margot is withdrawn and quiet, certainly in comparison with her animated sister, with whom she usually gets along quite well. They share a room until Fritz Pfeffer arrives at the end of 1942. Margot then sleeps in her parents' room. The fact that Anne and Peter are drawn to each other does not make Margot jealous, she tells Anne in a letter, but she regrets that she has no one 'with whom to share my thoughts and feelings'.[33]

Margot devotes herself mainly to her studies. She takes lessons in stenography and in all the normal school subjects. In November 1943 her father helps her select a correspondence course in Latin, and she registers in Bep's name. The instructor is very satisfied with his pupil: 'I take pleasure in your increasingly excellent work'.[34] Her Dutch is so good that she sometimes corrects Fritz Pfeffer's letters, and Anne calls her 'the Annexe's Dutch teacher'.[35] Like all the other Annexe occupants she reads a great deal.

Her household task is to help with the washing-up and with meal preparations, such as peeling potatoes. She also does various office chores. The first thing Margot wants to do after liberation is take a nice hot bath for at least half an hour. Her dream is to become a maternity nurse in Palestine, or perhaps even a doctor. Like Anne, Margot keeps a diary. Hers, however, has never been found.

MARGOT FRANK

In the Westerbork transit camp Margot meets an acquaintance from Amsterdam. They sleep in the same barracks and have a chat every now and then. Margot, Anne, their mother and Auguste van Pels are put in a barracks with about three hundred other women. Hopeful reports of the advancing Allies make the rounds in the camp, but the occupants of the Secret Annexe*, along with more than a thousand others, are selected for transport. After an uninterrupted journey of three days and nights in a bolted cattle car with more than sixty people, a modicum of fresh air and one bucket to serve as a toilet, Margot arrives in Auschwitz-Birkenau*.

She then undergoes the humiliation that turns her from a human being into a number: she must take off all her clothes, all her body hair is shaved off and a number is tattooed on her forearm. From early morning to late at night she is made to lug stones or cut turf. In late October or early November, she and Anne are selected for transport to Bergen-Belsen. Saying good-bye to their mother, who is left behind, must have been heartbreaking.

It's another journey under wretched conditions. If Auschwitz was an organized hell, Bergen-Belsen is a disorganized hell: there's hardly any food and little room for the many thousands of prisoners. The crematoria have broken down and dead bodies are lying about everywhere, so disease spreads rapidly.

Margot and Anne end up in a makeshift tent camp. After a few days a storm causes several of the tents to collapse, including theirs. They're moved to an overcrowded barracks. When a typhoid fever epidemic breaks out in the camp, Margot and Anne both succumb. In March 1945, only a few weeks before the camp is liberated by English troops, Margot dies. She is 19 years old.

ANNE FRANK

1942

NAME ——————————————— ANNELIES MARIE FRANK
BORN ————————————— 12 JUNE 1929
(FRANKFURT AM MAIN, GERMANY)
DIED ——————————— MARCH 1945
(BERGEN-BELSEN, GERMANY)

Johannes ——————————— '[...] a bright and intelligent
Kleiman, girl [...] with a strong desire
1953[36] to make something of
herself. She also had an
extraordinarily keen eye.'

Annelies Marie Frank is born on 12 June 1929. Anne's parents' home is on Marbachweg in a rather new part of Frankfurt. Anne spends her first years here in a comfortable house with a lovely garden. Gertrud Naumann, an older neighbour girl, and Kati Stilgenbauer, the live-in housekeeper, are only too happy to take care of the cheeky little toddler. Anne has no granddads, but she does have two grannies she's crazy about, along with five uncles, three aunties and two boy cousins. Anne is not physically strong and is often sick. In addition, her joints are too flexible, and when's she's a bit older her limbs will have a tendency to become dislocated. She has light brown flecked eyes, pretty dark hair and dimpled cheeks.

Anne is barely aware of the threatening situation and of her parents' decision to move to the Netherlands. She's just four years old when she (and Margot too at first) goes to stay with Granny Holländer in Aachen and later, in February 1934, is reunited with her parents and sister in Amsterdam. There Anne attends the Montessori* kindergarten. She makes many friends, including Hanneli Goslar, her neighbour on Merwedeplein. The *plein*, or square, is a children's paradise: whenever they want to play, the children go to each other's front door and whistle the same little tune.

From 1935 to 1941 Anne goes to the Montessori primary school, where she is an average pupil. Although her parents try to protect her from the menacing outside world, the now eleven-year-old Anne can't fail to notice that life for Jews is changing radically, certainly after May 1940 when all sorts of prohibitions come into effect. In 1941 she's required go to the Jewish Lyceum. In the classroom Anne is an incorrigible chatterbox, and on three different occasions she has to write an essay as punishment. The titles are 'A Chatterbox', 'An Incorrigible Chatterbox' and 'Quack, Quack, Quack Said Mistress Chatterback'.

Background
—
Cheeky little toddler

Flight to the Netherlands
—
Mistress Chatterback

> CONTINUED ON P. 64

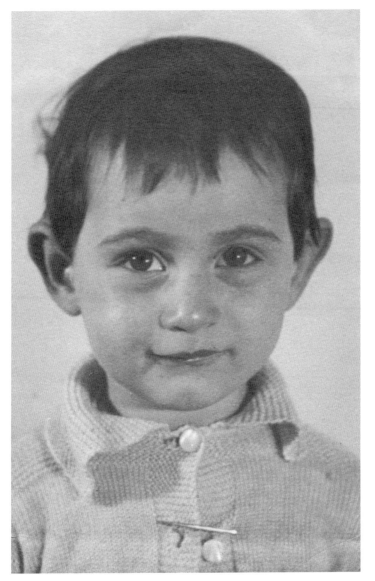

ANNE FRANK

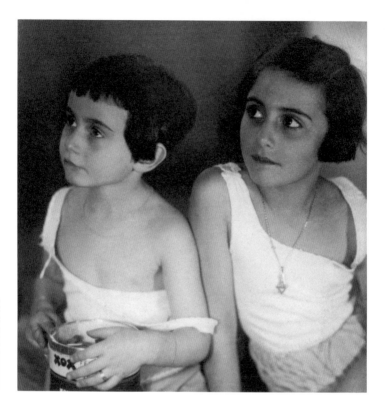

ANNE AND MARGOT,
AACHEN, 1933.

ANNE WITH HER
MOTHER AND MARGOT
IN SILS-MARIA,
SWITZERLAND, 1936.

ANNE (IN THE MIDDLE OF THE PHOTO AT THE BACK IN A WHITE DRESS) IN MISS BALDAL'S CLASS AT THE MONTESSORI SCHOOL IN AMSTERDAM, 1935.

ANNE PLAYING WITH HER GIRLFRIEND HANNELI GOSLAR ON MERWEDEPLEIN, MAY 1940.

ANNE'S TENTH
BIRTHDAY, 12 JUNE
1939. LEFT TO RIGHT:
LUCIE VAN DIJK,
ANNE, SANNE
LEDERMANN, HANNELI
GOSLAR, JUULTJE
KETELLAPPER, KÄTHE
EGYEDIE, MARY BOS,
IETJE SWILLENS
AND MARTHA VAN
DEN BERG.

ANNE AT HER WRITING
DESK, HOME ON
MERWEDEPLEIN,
MAY 1941.

ANNE FRANK

> CONTINUED FROM P. 56

Anne is a curious, outspoken child. She often plays ringleader and likes to boss people around. She loves games, skating, reading, movie stars, art and history. Writing will ultimately become her favourite hobby: on her 13th birthday she begins keeping a diary, and later she'll also start writing stories.

The first thing Anne puts in her bag when she hears they're going into hiding is her diary. It isn't until they're on their way that she learns where the hiding place is: the *achterhuis** of her father's office building on the Prinsengracht. In the two years that follow, Anne will rapidly grow from a child to a young woman. She develops keen powers of observation with regard to others and to herself. As the youngest member of the group in hiding she has a lot to put up with because everyone interferes in her upbringing. Like many adolescent girls, she has problems with her mother and is more drawn to her father. Her relationship with Margot gradually improves, however. In their second year in hiding she writes in her diary that she's in love with Peter. In the attic he gives her her first kiss – a clumsy one, but it's still an important moment!

During the day Anne works on her school assignments and stenography and does chores for the office. She also helps with the housekeeping: peeling potatoes, doing the washing-up and sweeping the rug. Like the others she reads stacks of books, including the girls' books that Mr Kleiman brings for her, and classic literature. She's also wild about the magazine *Cinema & Theater*, which Mr Kugler brings her on Mondays. Sometimes she chats with Bep about Bep's fiancé and the latest films. When she thinks about what she'd like to do after liberation she's 'so overjoyed'[37] she doesn't know where to begin, but she would really like to go back to school.

Time drags on monotonously and Anne longs more and more for nature, for 'fresh air and laughter'[38]. She follows the passing of seasons

In hiding
—
The dream of being a famous writer

ANNE FRANK

by looking at the big chestnut tree, which she can see from the attic window. Later Peter often joins her. Her diary, however, is still her greatest refuge: it's where she confides all her contradictory feelings, doubts and longings. Anne's dream is to become a famous journalist and writer. She takes her work very seriously: she writes stories and keeps a 'beautiful sentences' book with quotes from great writers and poets. On 20 May 1944 she begins rewriting her diary to make it suitable for publication after the war, a task she won't be able to finish.

When the raid takes place on 4 August 1944, SD* officer Karl Joseph Silberbauer needs a bag in which to put the confiscated valuables belonging to the occupants. He takes the briefcase containing Anne's precious diaries and shakes it out onto the floor. Her writings are left behind.

On the way to Westerbork, Anne 'would not move from the window,' Otto relates after the war. 'Outside, it was summer. Meadows, stubble fields, and villages flew by. [...] It was like freedom.'[39] After two years of confinement it's a relief for Anne to be outdoors again and to be able to talk to others.

In Auschwitz-Birkenau*, Anne is one of the youngest to survive the first selection. After a few weeks she comes down with scabies and is sent to the so-called *Krätzeblock**. Margot goes with her and Edith cares for them from outside as best she can. In late October or early November 1944, Anne and Margot are put on a transport to Bergen-Belsen. Edith Frank remains alone in Auschwitz-Birkenau: the selection system takes no account of family ties. Auguste van Pels may well have been on the same transport.

The living conditions are even worse in Bergen-Belsen. It's freezing cold and they're given almost nothing to eat. First they're assigned to a tent and later to a barracks. Anne and Margot have one of the worst spots right near the door where it's terribly draughty.

One evening Auguste van Pels comes to fetch Anne: her girlfriend Hanneli is in the adjoining camp! Anne meets Hanneli at the dividing wall, which is made of straw and barbed wire. They can't see each other, but they can hear each other's voices. Sad and happy at the same time, they exchange information. Anne thinks her parents are dead, 'and Margot is very sick too'.[40]

Hanneli, who is with her father and sister under slightly better conditions than Anne and Margot, will try to bring her a package of food the following evening. She succeeds, but when she throws the package over the fence another prisoner runs off with it. A few days later she tries again, and fortunately Anne catches the package herself. Dried fruits, crackers, a bit of food and warm socks: a precious treasure, but not enough to save her. Anne, like Margot, has contracted typhoid fever. When her sister dies in March, she has no one left. Soon Anne dies, 15 years old, of disease, exhaustion and despair.

HERMANN VAN PELS

1941

NAME	HERMANN VAN PELS
BORN	31 MARCH 1898
	(GEHRDE, GERMANY)
DIED	PROBABLY OCTOBER/NOVEMBER 1944
	(AUSCHWITZ, POLAND)
PSEUDONYM IN	HERMANN VAN DAAN
THE DIARY OF	
A YOUNG GIRL	

Anne Frank, 1943[41]

'...the man has a good head on his shoulders, but it's swelled to no small degree'.

Hermann is the fourth child of Aron van Pels and Lina Vorsänger. He has two brothers and three sisters. His paternal family were mostly butchers or dealers in butchers' equipment and were originally from Groningen in the Netherlands. This is why Hermann has Dutch nationality, even though he was born in Gehrde in Germany.

After secondary school he moves from Kiel to Hamburg and then to Osnabrück. In the latter city he serves as an apprentice in a department store for three years, according to one of his sisters. On 25 December 1925 he marries Auguste Röttgen, and almost one year later their son Peter is born. From 6 September 1930 to 26 June 1937 Hermann, Auguste and Peter live in Martinistraße in Osnabrück. He works as a sales representative for butchers' equipment, travelling around the area with his father. He sees his relatives regularly in his parents' big house in Gehrde. As the years pass, Hermann turns his attention to business, focusing on a range of merchandise: meat, herbs and textiles.

In 1937 Hermann van Pels moves to Amsterdam with his wife and son. His father follows in 1938 after *Kristallnacht**, with one suitcase in hand. Eventually one brother and all three sisters will come here to live. Hermann is hired by Otto Frank's company Pectacon as a specialist in herbs and spices. According to Miep Gies, 'with one sniff of his nose he could name any spice'. [42] He and Otto come up with ideas for selling new products and increasing the clientele.

Hermann lives in Amsterdam at several addresses and finally ends up at 34-II Zuider Amstellaan. Their home is right behind Merwedeplein, where the Frank family live. Hermann and Auguste occasionally visit the Franks on Saturdays for coffee. Hermann is a big man, very outgoing. He 'always had a moment for a joke'. [43]

Background
—
**Dutch
nationality**

Flight to the
Netherlands
—
**Specialist
in herbs
and spices**

> CONTINUED ON P. 73

HERMANN (LEFT) WITH
VICTOR KUGLER ON
THE DAY OF THE
WEDDING OF MIEP AND
JAN GIES, 16 JULY 1941.

ABOVE:
MARTINISTRASSE IN
OSNABRÜCK, WHERE
THE VAN PELS FAMILY
LIVED FROM 1930 UNTIL
THEIR DEPARTURE FOR
THE NETHERLANDS.

BELOW: HERMANN
AND AUGUSTE (FAR
LEFT AND FAR RIGHT)
WITH ANOTHER
COUPLE, OSNABRÜCK,
AROUND 1930.

SHOPPING LIST DURING THE HIDING PERIOD, WRITTEN BY HERMANN: '3 COUPONS TO BE CREDITED; 2 COUPONS FOR LIVER SAUSAGE, 1 COUPON FOR BLOOD SAUSAGE'. THE ORDER READS AS FOLLOWS: '1½ BLOOD SAUSAGE AND 1½ LIVER SAUSAGE, CALVES' FEET OR SMALL HEAD'.

HERMANN
SURROUNDED BY
THE FEMALE STAFF AT
OPEKTA/PECTACON:
LEFT TO RIGHT:
ESTHER, BEP AND MIEP,
MAY 1941.

> CONTINUED FROM P. 68

In hiding
—
Shortage of funds

In 1942 Otto and Hermann decide to turn the *achterhuis** of the office building into a hiding place for both families, just to be on the safe side. Over the next few months they secretly stock it with furniture, household goods and food. Hermann takes Miep with him a few times to a butcher in the Jordaan district of Amsterdam (Miep is not yet in on the scheme). When the Van Pels family go into hiding on 13 July 1942, Hermann assures Miep that she'll be able to buy meat there herself: 'He's a good friend of mine. You'll see, he'll give you what you want if he can.'[44] After one particularly large purchase, Hermann dons his wife's apron and makes a whole range of sausages. He often spends evenings working for the business in the warehouse, where the herb mixtures are prepared.

Because Hermann and Auguste have no ration registration cards* they have to spend a great deal of money on food. Hermann has to sell more and more of their possessions on the black market. Jo Kleiman does this for him. This leads to many a quarrel with his 'Kerli', as he calls Auguste, with both of them swearing and screaming at each other. But they always make up, and he never fails to give his wife a bouquet of red carnations on her birthday. Hermann likes to talk politics with the men and discuss developments on the front. Armed with the inevitable cigarette, he sits glued to the radio and doesn't miss a single broadcast. He is pessimistic about the outcome.

After discovery
—
A fatal injury

At Camp Westerbork the men and women live apart. Hermann and Peter van Pels stay together, and in the evening they're able to chat a bit with Auguste. On Saturday evening, 2 September 1944, all eight are selected for transport to Auschwitz*. Immediately after arriving at Auschwitz-Birkenau the men are separated from the women for good: Hermann will never see Auguste again. Hermann, Peter, Otto Frank and Fritz Pfeffer are put to work in Auschwitz I.

HERMANN VAN PELS

73

According to Otto Frank, Herman seriously
injures his thumb a few weeks later and asks
permission to work indoors until it is healed.
When a selection is made by the camp guards,
the injured Hermann is chosen and led away along
with a group of other men. Otto and Peter watch
him go.

On an unknown day, probably in October or
November 1944, Herman van Pels is killed.
He is 46 years old.

AUGUSTE VAN PELS

1941

NAME	AUGUSTE VAN PELS-RÖTTGEN
BORN	29 SEPTEMBER 1900 (BUER, GERMANY)
DIED	APRIL 1945 (GERMANY OR CZECHOSLOVAKIA)
PSEUDONYM IN *THE DIARY OF A YOUNG GIRL*	PETRONELLA VAN DAAN

Victor Kugler describing the role of Auguste in a play in New York, 1956[45]

'Unlike the others, she [...] is remarkably well-groomed with a nice hair-do, make-up, etc., etc. It's all another way of underscoring her totally different character.'

On 29 September 1900, Auguste Röttgen is born in Buer, which today is part of Gelsenkirchen in the German state of North Rhine-Westphalia. Her parents are Leo Röttgen and Rosa Rosenau, and Auguste has four sisters. Nothing is known about Auguste's educational history.

On her 25th birthday she marries Hermann van Pels in Elberfeld, her place of residence, and thereby acquires Dutch nationality. She goes to live with him in Osnabrück. On 8 November 1926 their son Peter is born. From September 1930 to June 1937, she and her family live on Martinistraße and are enrolled at the orthodox synagogue. Auguste, also known as Gusti, is a good housewife and takes care of Peter. She loves to talk – and at length. She's an elegant and coquettish lady who is conscious of her appearance and fond of pretty clothes.

In July 1937, Auguste, Hermann and Peter van Pels leave Germany for Amsterdam. Because of their Dutch nationality they have no trouble emigrating. They take their furniture and other valuables with them. After living in an upstairs flat on Stadionweg, they move into a house on Biesboschstraat, where her parents live with them from late March to early September 1939. Like many people at that time, she sometimes rents a room to acquaintances or refugees. In May 1940 the Van Pels family move to a spacious four-room flat on Zuider Amstellaan. Peter attends school and plays soccer with boys in the neighbourhood. Occasionally they all go to visit the Frank family. Relatives of Auguste emigrate to America, but she herself never succeeds in getting beyond the Netherlands. On 13 July 1942 she and her family leave their home to go into hiding.

Auguste's household task in the Secret Annexe* is that of cook, a role that suits her to a T. Making something out of the increasingly monotonous and meagre rations requires quite a bit of conjuring. Auguste sometimes interferes with the way Anne and Margot are being raised, which she regards as too liberal. This rubs Edith Frank the wrong way.

Background
—
Coquettish and elegant

Flight to the Netherlands
—
Stranded in the Netherlands

In hiding
—
Keeping things lively

> CONTINUED ON P. 81

AUGUSTE,
AROUND 1920.

AUGUSTE WITH HER
MOTHER AND FOUR
SISTERS; AUGUSTE IS
PROBABLY ON THE
FAR RIGHT.

AUGUSTE VAN PELS

AUGUSTE, 16 JULY 1941.

79

LEFT TO RIGHT:
TWO UNIDENTIFIED
PERSONS, AUGUSTE
AND HERMANN VAN
PELS AND VICTOR
KUGLER AT THE
WEDDING OF MIEP AND
JAN GIES, 16 JULY 1941.

ZUIDER AMSTELLAAN
(NOW ROOSEVELT-
LAAN), WHERE THE
VAN PELS FAMILY LIVED
AT NUMBER 34, WITH
DANIËL WILLINKPLEIN
TO THE RIGHT (NOW
VICTORIEPLEIN) AND
THE WOLKENKRABBER
(THE FIRST

RESIDENTIAL TOWER
BLOCK IN
AMSTERDAM).
MERWEDEPLEIN,
WHERE THE FRANK
FAMILY LIVED, IS
BEHIND THE
WOLKENKRABBER,
ABOUT 1932.

> CONTINUED FROM P. 76

After a few months their relationship cools, all the more so when the Franks discover that Auguste has been withholding food. She gets into fierce rows with Hermann, whom she endearingly calls 'Putti', and she loves flirting with the other men. Auguste keeps things lively. She's a great talker and enjoys a good laugh, but as the months in hiding drag on, she, like Edith Frank, becomes increasingly despondent and sombre.

The Van Pels family are gradually forced to sell all their possessions to buy food, and Auguste parts with her beautiful fur coat – with difficulty. Yet she does make a very generous gesture during that difficult period: in February 1944, Auguste gives Miep Gies an antique ring for her birthday with the words, 'This is just a small token of our appreciation and friendship'.[46]

After discovery
—
A brutal death

After the arrest and transport to Camp Westerbork, Auguste and the other female prisoners are made to dismantle batteries, a filthy and dangerous business. At five o'clock in the morning the workday begins. Seated at long tables, the women break open batteries in order to remove the carbon rods. Then they pick out the sticky brown mass, which contains poisonous ammonium chloride. Finally all the components are collected separately for use in the war industry. In early September, among the 1,019 names that are read aloud for what proves to be the last transport from Westerbork to Auschwitz-Birkenau* is that of Auguste. In the chaos that ensues on the train platform at Auschwitz she is heartlessly separated from her son and husband. Auguste makes it through the first selection for the gas chambers. During the day she does hard labour and at night she sleeps with more than a thousand other women in a barracks originally meant for 52 horses.

In October or November 1944, Auguste is put on a transport to Bergen-Belsen, probably along with Margot and Anne. She stays there for a few months. Hanneli Goslar, a friend of Anne's, later reports that she encountered Auguste van Pels at

AUGUSTE VAN PELS

the fence. Auguste recognized her name and said right away, 'Oh, you'll want to speak with Anne'.[47] Auguste helped the two friends get back in touch with each other.

In February 1945 Auguste is deported to Raguhn, an *Außenlager** of the Buchenwald concentration camp, and several weeks later to Theresienstadt. As eyewitness Rachel van Amerongen-Frankfoorder later reports, Auguste is brutally murdered on that last transport: the Nazis throw her under the train and she dies on the spot. She is 44 years old.

AUGUSTE VAN PELS

PETER
VAN PELS

1942

NAME	PETER VAN PELS
BORN	8 NOVEMBER 1926 (OSNABRÜCK, GERMANY)
DIED	PROBABLY SECOND HALF OF APRIL 1945 (MAUTHAUSEN, AUSTRIA)
PSEUDONYM IN *THE DIARY OF A YOUNG GIRL*	PETER VAN DAAN

Anne Frank, 1944[48]

'Peter is peace-loving, tolerant and extremely easygoing.

Peter is born in Osnabrück not far from the Dutch border, the only child of Auguste Röttgen and Hermann van Pels. Peter acquires Dutch nationality through his father. Speaking of his youth in Osnabrück, a neighbour boy from Martinstraße remembers playing with Peter and other local children in the street: they ride on scooters, play with marbles and play hide-and-seek and tag. His father comes home for lunch and brings Peter inside to eat with him.

Peter attends the Jewish school on Roland-straße, next to the synagogue. He plays sports on the vacant lot behind the school with a small group of friends; according to one of them Peter and another boy are 'the best soccer players'.[49] Peter has thick dark hair and beautiful blue eyes. He is quiet and shy. Because he attends a Jewish school, he sees his classes growing smaller and smaller as many families flee Germany.

Peter van Pels is ten when he and his parents emigrate to Amsterdam. He often visits his granddad Aron van Pels and his Aunt Henny. A cousin of Hermann later recalls that Peter was very good with his hands and often did little carpentry jobs.

For Peter, emigrating means a new school, new friends and learning a new language. He spends a few months in a class where German-Jewish children are given lessons in Dutch and in assimilating into Dutch society. After primary school he enters the Spinoza School (a MULO*) in the Rivierenbuurt, a district of Amsterdam. In 1941, when Peter is required to attend a Jewish school, he probably takes up vocational training where he learns such things as furniture upholstery.

One week after the Frank family move into the Secret Annexe*, Peter arrives with his parents and his cat Mouschi. He is 15 years old. Peter is given the little room with the stairs leading up to the attic. He's the only one in the group with a room of his own room, to which he often retreats.

Background
—
Smaller and smaller classes

Flight to the Netherlands
—
Good with his hands

In hiding
—
Hunger and dreaming of freedom

> CONTINUED ON P. 91

PETER WORKING ON
THE SPRINGS OF A
CHAIR, BETWEEN MAY
AND JULY 1942. THE
JEWISH STAR* CAN BE
SEEN ON THE LEFT
BREAST POCKET OF
HIS OVERALLS.

PETER VAN PELS

PETER (SECOND
FROM THE LEFT)
WITH THE CHILDREN
AND NANNY OF THE
JACOBSONS, FAMILY
FRIENDS, SUMMER OF
1927 OR 1928.

CLASS PHOTO OF
THE ISRAELITISCHE
ELEMENTARSCHULE
IN OSNABRÜCK,
1934. PETER IS IN THE
THIRD ROW, SECOND
FROM THE LEFT, IN
THE CLASS TAUGHT BY
ABRAHAM TREPP.

BECAUSE SO MANY
CHILDREN WERE
EMIGRATING,
A FAREWELL PHOTO
WAS TAKEN OF SOME

BOYS FROM PETER'S
CLASS, AROUND 1936.
PETER IS IN THE
MIDDLE.

THE ATTIC OF THE
SECRET ANNEXE,
WHERE PETER AND
ANNE LIKE TO SIT;
THEY LOOK THROUGH
THE WINDOW AT
THE CHESTNUT TREE.

THE STOCK MARKET
GAME THAT PETER IS
GIVEN ON 8 NOVEMBER
1942 FOR HIS 16TH
BIRTHDAY. HE PLAYS
WITH IT OFTEN.

> CONTINUED FROM P. 84

There's just enough room for his bed, a small table and a chair. His bicycle hangs on the wall.

Peter's chore in the Secret Annexe is to haul up the potatoes and vegetables delivered to the warehouse by the greengrocer. He chops wood, does most of the carpentry work and takes care of Mouschi. He builds a small workshop in the loft where he can potter about. He also likes to do crossword puzzles. He is not a fearful lad: when burglars are detected, Peter goes downstairs with the other men (and a heavy hammer) to size up the situation. And he demonstrates resolve when he twice retrieves a book that his parents have declared off-limits.

As a growing boy, he must have been constantly hungry in the Secret Annexe. In her diary Anne reports that 'even after the most substantial meal' he 'could have eaten twice as much'.[50]

Like Anne and Margot, Peter is studying stenography as well as various school subjects, including English, French, Dutch and history. Otto often helps him with his studies. Peter sees himself as a good-for-nothing, he tells Anne during one of their confidential talks in the attic. Later he wants to go to the Dutch East Indies (today's Indonesia) to live on the plantations. But the first thing he wants to do when he is free again is go downtown and take in a movie!

PETER VAN PELS

After discovery
—
Death march of more than 500 kilometres

On 4 August 1944, Peter is sitting in the attic with Otto Frank going over an English lesson when the Sicherheitsdienst* bursts into the Secret Annexe. After the arrest, Peter is sent to Camp Westerbork and finally ends up in the men's barracks in Auschwitz I*, along with his father, Otto Frank and Fritz Pfeffer. Peter is lucky, he is put to work in the mail department, which gives him access to many different parts of the camp. Sometimes he's able to procure extra food, which he can pass on to his father, Fritz and the weakened Otto.

After only a few weeks, Peter and Otto witness Peter's father being led away with a small group of men.

'And I shall never forget how in Auschwitz the 17-year-old Peter [...] and I saw a group of men being selected,' Otto later recalls. 'One of them was Peter's father'.[51]

In January 1945 the guards clear the camp to escape the approaching Russian army. Otto implores Peter to hide, but he refuses. He is taken along on a brutal trek that ends at the Mauthausen concentration camp in Austria and will later become known as one of the infamous death marches*. In the Melk *Außenlager** at Mauthausen he is put to work doing very heavy mining for the construction of an underground ball bearing factory. The prisoners are given no medical care whatsoever and live under barbarous conditions. Peter is finally put in the *Sanitätslager* (sick barracks) of the main camp where he dies of exhaustion, probably in the second half of April 1945. He is 18 years old. Shortly afterwards – on 5 May – the camp is liberated.

PETER VAN PELS

FRITZ PFEFFER

1937 OR 1938

NAME	FRITZ PFEFFER
BORN	30 APRIL 1889
	(GIESSEN, GERMANY)
DIED	20 DECEMBER 1944
	(NEUENGAMME, GERMANY)
PSEUDONYM IN *THE DIARY OF A YOUNG GIRL*	ALBERT DUSSEL

Alfred Sand, childhood friend of Fritz's son Werner in Berlin, 1995[52]

'He was strict and even a perfectionist, but he was also friendly.'

Fritz Pfeffer is born on 30 April 1889 in Gießen, a city about 50 kilometres north of Frankfurt am Main. He is one of six children born into a religious Jewish family. His father is a textile merchant and his parents own a clothing shop in the centre of the city. Gießen lies in the midst of several rivers, streams and lakes, and it is here that Fritz discovers his love of water. He enjoys swimming and rowing as well as walking and horseback riding.

He completes gymnasium and goes on to study medicine in Würzburg, where he takes technical and theoretical courses in dentistry. This is probably followed by a degree in dentistry in Berlin. In 1913, at the age of 24, he opens his own practice in Berlin-Charlottenburg. He spends his free time rowing to his heart's content in the watery areas surrounding the city. He is also a member of Berlin's Undine rowing society.

During the First World War, Fritz Pfeffer fights in the 116th infantry regiment and is involved in the bloody and infamous Battle of Verdun and the Battle of the Somme. After the war he resumes his successful dentistry practice. In 1926 he marries Vera Henriette Bythiner, and in April 1927 their son Werner is born. After their divorce in 1933, Fritz raises Werner on his own. He is a strict and disciplined father. Religion is important to him. Werner later says that his father celebrated every Jewish holiday and observed all the Jewish laws.

In around 1935 he meets his great love, the Catholic Charlotte Kaletta. They cannot marry because the Nuremberg racial laws* have banned mixed marriages. Both of them love animals, especially horses, and they enjoy going on excursions. Fritz is always immaculately dressed, usually in a smart suit.

In 1938, with Nazi Germany becoming more and more threatening, Fritz Pfeffer decides to at least ensure the safety of his son. He finds Werner a place on a boat bound for England, where his brother Ernst will care for him.

Background
—
A sport-loving dentist

Flight to the Netherlands
—
Dutch tolerance

> CONTINUED ON P. 101

FRITZ IN MILITARY
SERVICE DURING THE
FIRST WORLD WAR,
1917.

FRITZ (CENTRE) WITH
TWO BROTHERS,
AROUND 1910.

THE SHOP WITH
LADIES' AND
CHILDREN'S CLOTHING
RUN BY FRITZ'S
PARENTS IN GIESSEN.

FRITZ ON HORSEBACK,
PROBABLY DURING
THE TWENTIES.

FRITZ (CENTRE) IN
A ROWBOAT DURING
THE THIRTIES.

FRITZ PFEFFER

FRITZ WITH HIS SON
WERNER, 1937 OR 1938.
WERNER SURVIVES THE
WAR AND MOVES TO
THE US, WHERE HE
TAKES THE NAME PETER
PEPPER. HE DIES
IN 1995.

FRITZ WITH
CHARLOTTE KALETTA,
AROUND 1940.

16. VI. 1943.

Mijn reis door Nederland.

uit het Spaans vertaald door

Fredo.

De reis beschrijving door Nederland van den
beroemden Spaansen schrijver W. Fernández Flórez
is zo levendig en schilderachtig uit het jaar 1928,
dat wij ze nog eens weergeven. Het boekje bezit een
zo grote weelderigheid en — wij durven het uit te spreken —
een zulke nauwkeurigheid van waarneming, dat
het een teken van slechste smaak zou zijn, te
proberen, ook maar iets te verbeteren.

16. VI. 1943.

> CONTINUED FROM P. 94

Fritz himself cannot go along; because of the huge flood of refugees England is taking only a limited number of Jews, mainly children.

After *Kristallnacht**, Fritz and Charlotte flee to the Netherlands. Even though Pfeffer is unable to obtain a residence permit, he is not sent back. The frustrating thing is that he and Charlotte are not allowed to marry in the Netherlands either without the permission of the German government. Fritz tries to escape to Australia, Aruba or Chile. Their preference is Chile, where he and Charlotte dream of breeding horses. But Fritz's request to await the emigration application in the Netherlands is rejected. While his presence in the Netherlands is tolerated, he does not have official permission to work there. He occasionally does some illegal work for Samuel van der Hoeden, a dental technician. In May 1940 Fritz Pfeffer meets Otto Frank, and he and Charlotte join the group of refugees and friends who spend Saturday afternoons at the Frank's Merwedeplein flat. There Fritz also meets Miep and Jan Gies and the Van Pels family.

In hiding

—

Love at a distance

In late 1942, Fritz asks Miep (who is his patient) whether she knows of a possible hiding place. Miep presents his request to the Frank and Van Pels families and to the other helpers before smuggling Fritz into the Secret Annexe*. The occupants greet him with coffee and cognac. He is speechless with amazement: he thought the Franks had fled to Switzerland.

At 53, Pfeffer is the oldest occupant of the Secret Annexe (he's two weeks older than Otto). He has to share a room with the adolescent Anne, who has covered the walls with photos and pictures. An athletic man, he must have felt very cooped up in the Annexe. He's the only one without a family or loved one at his side, so he feels quite alone. He has frequent run-ins with the others. Miep serves as the messenger between Fritz and his beloved, who write to each other regularly.

FRITZ PFEFFER

Charlotte does not know how close Fritz's hiding place is, and she sometimes give Miep packages containing food and books. Anne writes that he usually keeps the tasty things for himself.

Fritz reads a great deal during the day. He also studies Spanish, ever hopeful about the Chilean horse breeding farm. In the evenings he likes to study in the quiet of Kugler's office, or to write letters to his 'Lotte'. Like the other, he helps with peeling potatoes and washing-up, and of course he's the house dentist and doctor.

Fritz too is transported via Camp Westerbork to Auschwitz I*, where he is forced to do hard labour. Road construction is one of his tasks. The prisoners are literally worked to death for the benefit of the German war industry. In October 1944, Fritz Pfeffer is included in a transport of physicians and dentists being sent to the Neuengamme concentration camp near Hamburg. He may have volunteered for this, hoping that conditions there would be an improvement over Auschwitz. This movement of prisoners to other camps has to do with the Allied advance in late 1944, when the Nazis are feeling mounting pressure to erase all traces of their atrocities. Fritz survives the transport but dies in Neuengamme on 20 December of illness, deprivation and exhaustion.

After discovery
—
Worked to death

JOHANNES KLEIMAN

AROUND 1950.

NAME	—————————————	JOHANNES KLEIMAN
BORN	—————————————	17 AUGUST 1896
		(KOOG AAN DE ZAAN, THE NETHERLANDS)
DIED	—————————————	28 JANUARY 1959
		(AMSTERDAM, THE NETHERLANDS)
PSEUDONYM IN	—————————————	MR KOOPHUIS
THE DIARY OF		
A YOUNG GIRL		

Edith Frank, —————————— **'When Mr Kleiman enters**
according to **a room, the sun begins**
Anne Frank, **to shine.'**
1943[53]

Johannes Kleiman is born in 1896 in Koog aan de Zaan, the Netherlands. His family is Dutch Reformed, but religion plays only a minor role in Johannes's life. Jo, as he is usually called, may have been trained as an office worker. He is a 'frail-looking, pale-faced man with [...] a delicate look'.[54] On 12 July 1923 he marries Johanna Catharina Reuman, and in 1927 their daughter Johanna is born. The family are also known as Jo, Jo and Jo. Kleiman meets Otto Frank at about the same time. Otto has set up a branch of the Frankfurt family bank in Amsterdam and makes Kleiman assignee with power of attorney*. Their friendship grows with the years and they become co-workers. In 1933 Otto is appointed to the supervisory board of the Central Trade and Industry Association, a company of which Kleiman is director. Kleiman and his brother Willy are also involved in other businesses: they own CIMEX, a pest control company, and both are on the supervisory board of N.V. Paauwe's Fully Automatic Timepieces, which manufactures clocks. Jo Kleiman is a jack-of-all-trades.

Jo Kleiman plays an important role in the creation of Pectacon in 1938 and becomes its director. This is where he meets the spice specialist Hermann van Pels. After the forced Aryanization* of the companies in 1941, Kleiman is appointed director of Otto Frank's N.V. Opekta company. Pectacon is closed down, but its activities are taken up by a new company, Gies & Co, under the direction of Victor Kugler. Kleiman works in the office on the Prinsengracht, along with Miep and Bep. In his scarce free time he enjoys walking and bicycling. He has a trustworthy, peaceful personality, but his health is a problem: his stomach often acts up on him.

Jo Kleiman points out to Otto Frank that the building's *achterhuis** would be a very good place for his family (and the Van Pels family) to go into hiding. It has a kitchen and a toilet and can therefore function quite independently – with the help of people from the office.

> CONTINUED ON P. 111

JOHANNES NEXT TO
THE REVOLVING
BOOKCASE, 1954.

JOHANNES (LEFT)
WITH VICTOR KUGLER
AT THE DOOR OF 263
PRINSENGRACHT,
EARLY FIFTIES.

JOHANNES WITH
TWO VISITORS
IN THE ATTIC OF
THE SECRET ANNEXE,
AROUND 1955.

EMPLOYEES AND THEIR FAMILIES IN THE NEW OPEKTA BUILDING ON VAN SLINGELANDT-STRAAT, 7 MAY 1955. STANDING ON THE FAR LEFT IS JAN GIES, WITH FRITZI AND OTTO FRANK SITTING IN FRONT OF HIM. SEATED IN THE MIDDLE FOREGROUND IS JOHANNA KLEIMAN; BESIDE HER TO THE RIGHT IS JOHANNES WITH THEIR GRANDDAUGHTER. BEHIND THEM ARE MIEP GIES, LOES KUGLER, CHARLOTTE KALETTA AND OTHERS.

JOHANNES WITH HIS
WIFE (LEFT) VISITING
OTTO AND FRITZI IN
SWITZERLAND DURING
THE FIFTIES.

> CONTINUED FROM P. 104

Kleiman and his brother Willy, who has a lorry, help transport furniture to the hiding place. His wife Johanna is aware of the situation and occasionally accompanies him on his visits there. When Auguste van Pels is forced to sell her rabbit fur coat for badly needed cash, Johanna Kleiman peddles it on the black market; she thinks her husband is less suited to hawking a lady's fur coat.

During an infestation of fleas in the Secret Annexe*, Kleiman's knowledge of pest control comes in very handy: 'Mr Kleiman sprinkled yellow powder in every nook and cranny'.[55] He also sometimes brings along his daughter's books for Anne to read. The stress involved in keeping eight Annexe occupants safely hidden won't have done Kleiman's sensitive stomach any good. Then there are the several office break-ins, and the day the new owner (Otto rented the property) suddenly comes to examine the building and Kleiman has to make up an excuse about forgetting the key to the *achterhuis* door...

Yet he tries to cheer up the occupants as best he can and to bring them bits of information every day. He keeps the worst things to himself to avoid upsetting them, but reports of the concentration camps and the Nazi atrocities slip in via the radio.

During the hiding period Kleiman maintains written contact with Otto Frank's brother-in-law in Basel, Erich Elias. These are impersonal reports from which the family in Switzerland may be able to deduce how the people in hiding are doing by reading between the lines: 'Just a few lines to let you know that we are all doing well'.[56]

After discovery
—
Intense involvement with the Anne Frank House

On 4 August 1944, Jo Kleiman finds himself sitting next to Otto Frank at the police station. Otto whispers how distressed he is that the helpers should have been arrested for what the Annexe occupants have done. 'Don't give it another thought,' Kleiman answers. 'It was up to me, and I wouldn't have done it any differently.'[57]

JOHANNES KLEIMAN

Kleiman and Kugler are lucky that most of the war's battles have been fought by August 1944 and the Germans are beginning to have doubts about a successful outcome. The two men are sent to a house of detention and then to Camp Amersfoort. At the intervention of the Red Cross, Jo Kleiman is allowed to go home after a few weeks on account of his stomach ailment.

He resumes his activities at Opekta. After the war, he and Otto Frank try to set up a new business. Kleiman is also intensely involved in the publication of the diary and the creation of the Anne Frank House; he represents Otto Frank on the board of directors, since Otto travels a great deal. He also regularly gives tours of the building, which becomes more widely known after the diary is published.

At the age of 63 Johannes Kleiman suffers a fatal heart attack at his desk at Opekta. Otto Frank speaks at his funeral.

VICTOR KUGLER

1930

NAME	VICTOR GUSTAV KUGLER
BORN	6 JUNE 1900
	(HOHENELBE, AUSTRIA-HUNGARY;
	TODAY'S CZECH REPUBLIC)
DIED	14 DECEMBER 1981
	(TORONTO, CANADA)
PSEUDONYM IN	MR KRALER
THE DIARY OF	
A YOUNG GIRL	

Inscription in the book *Weerklank van Anne Frank*[58] — 'For Mr Kugler, in remembrance of everything he did for me and my family during our time in hiding. In old solidarity, Otto Frank, 26 April 1970.'

VICTOR KUGLER

Victor Kugler is born on 6 June 1900, the son of an unmarried seamstress, Emilie Kugler. In around 1909 Emilie marries Franz Klose. The three go to live in Duisburg, where Victor is eventually joined by two half-brothers and two half-sisters. In primary school Victor is a good pupil, and in 1914, after secondary school, he returns to his birthplace to attend a vocational school and learn the weaver's trade. He probably stays with family members still living there, or finds accommodation elsewhere.

He is too young to be called up when the First World War starts, but when he turns 17 he is drafted into the Austrian navy. In 1918 he is wounded and released from service.

After the war he works at several different jobs: as an electrician in a mine and as a mechanic for the Deutsche Maschinenfabrik, among others. While working for the last company he is sent to Utrecht for an assembly job. He seizes this opportunity to escape from the dreary mining region of his youth and work his way up from electrician to office clerk. He obtains his diploma in Dutch Commercial Correspondence and meets Laua Maria (Marie) Buntenbach, whom he marries on 2 February 1928. Kugler goes to work for Frans van Angeren, the owner of a patisserie/lunchroom and importer of baking ingredients. This puts him in touch with the pectin trade and Opekta.

Kugler's favourite hobby is photography. He owns a good camera, a Leica, and occasionally he wins prizes with submissions to photo contests. He is also fond of motorcycling, classical music, walking and birdwatching. He is a slender man with dark hair and light blue eyes. Victor always dresses impeccably and is formal, calm and modest.

In 1933 his work for Van Angeren brings Victor Kugler into contact with Otto Frank, who has recently set up his own branch of Opekta. Kugler goes to work for Opekta and moves to Hilversum with his wife. He handles the company's orders, among other things, and is interested in the possibilities that pectin has to offer the food industry.

> CONTINUED ON P. 119

VICTOR HOLDING
HIS LEICA CAMERA,
16 JULY 1941.

VICTOR WITH HIS
MOTHER EMILIE, 1909.

VICTOR AS A SAILOR IN
THE AUSTRIAN NAVY,
1917 OR 1918.

VICTOR (SECOND FROM THE RIGHT) RECEIVES THE YAD VASHEM AWARD. ON THE LEFT IS HIS SECOND WIFE LOES, AND NEXT TO HER IS THE ISRAELI AMBASSADOR TO CANADA, 1973.

VICTOR MAINTAINS CONTACT WITH OTTO AND FRITZI; THIS IS THE THREE OF THEM IN AMSTERDAM, AROUND 1970.

VICTOR KUGLER

VICTOR KUGLER

VICTOR (SECOND FROM THE RIGHT) RECEIVES THE YAD VASHEM AWARD. ON THE LEFT IS HIS SECOND WIFE LOES, AND NEXT TO HER IS THE ISRAELI AMBASSADOR TO CANADA, 1973.

VICTOR MAINTAINS CONTACT WITH OTTO AND FRITZI; THIS IS THE THREE OF THEM IN AMSTERDAM, AROUND 1970.

118

> CONTINUED FROM P. 114

To this end he carries out chemical tests in the company kitchen.

When it becomes impossible for Otto Frank, as a Jew, to run and own his businesses, Pectacon's operations are taken over by a new company, Gies & Co, with Kugler as director. In 1942, Otto Frank asks Kugler if he would help Otto's family and that of his colleague Van Pels, should they decide to go into hiding. He agrees without hesitation. 'I had to. They were my friends,' he later says.[59]

In hiding
—
Mastermind of the bookcase

Once the Frank and Van Pels families are safely hidden, Kugler comes up with the idea of placing a revolving bookcase in front of the door leading to the Secret Annexe*. He is afraid that the Germans might come looking for hidden bicycles. With a bookcase in front of the door, the Secret Annexe would be better protected from strangers. Warehouse supervisor Johannes Voskuijl, Bep's father, builds the bookcase. Kugler and Kleiman keep the businesses going during the hiding period. Kugler sometimes sells consignments of spices off the books to provide the Annexe occupants with more money.

During lunch breaks, when the warehouse workers are out, Victor goes upstairs to talk with the Secret Annexe occupants. He often brings them newspapers and magazines. Anne especially looks forward to his Monday visits, when he arrives with the latest issue of *Cinema & Theater*. He later will recall her eager expression: 'I would hide it in my pocket, so that I could watch those questioning eyes for longer'.[60]

Victor's wife knows nothing about his illegal activities, so he is unable to share the stress that comes with this responsibility.

After discovery
—
Emigrating to Canada

'Mitgefangen, mitgehangen'[61]: imprisoned together, hung together! These are the words that are used to threaten Kugler and Kleiman during their first interrogation in the SD* building. As a helper of Jews, Kugler is sent to three Dutch camps: Amersfoort (from which the sick Kleiman is released), Zwolle and Wageningen.

In Camp Zwolle, Kugler makes contact with Martin Brouwer, a sales representative for Gies & Co, who acts as a guarantor for the prisoner. Victor is permitted to spend his nights at Brouwer's home, but during the day he has to work in the camp. With his homemade vermicelli and improvised oil lamps, Victor Kugler is a big hit with Brouwer's children.

On around 28 March 1945, Kugler and six hundred other prisoners are put on a forced march from Wageningen to Germany. The column comes under fire along the way, and in the chaos that ensues Victor manages to escape by running into a field. After days of wandering, and with the help of several strangers and a false identification card, he finally reaches his home in Hilversum and his wife Marie. He's able to hide there until liberation in May 1945.

After liberation, Victor Kugler goes back to work at Opekta. In 1952 Marie dies. In 1953 Victor marries a new Opekta employee, Loes van Langen, and together they emigrate to Canada in 1955. There he works as an electrician and insurance agent. They live on a modest income. He maintains contact with his friends in Amsterdam and writes Otto an enthusiastic and detailed account of the play *The Diary of Anne Frank*, which he attends in 1956 in New York. Referring to the actor Josef Schildkraut, who plays Otto Frank, Kugler writes, 'His bearing, manner of speech and gestures are all just like yours.'[62] After retiring, he gives a series of lectures on the history of the Secret Annexe and the diary, which has now become famous in Canada as well. He contracts Alzheimer's disease and dies in 1981 at the age of 81 in a hospital in Toronto.

BEP VOSKUIJL

1937

NAME	ELISABETH VAN WIJK-VOSKUIJL
BORN	5 JULY 1919
	(AMSTERDAM, THE NETHERLANDS)
DIED	6 MAY 1983
	(AMSTERDAM, THE NETHERLANDS)
PSEUDONYM IN *THE DIARY OF A YOUNG GIRL*	ELLI VOSSEN

Bep Voskuijl, 1957[63]

'[...] I'm not what you would call a "woman of the world".'

Elisabeth – usually called Bep – is the oldest daughter of Johannes Voskuijl and Christine Sodenkamp. She is born in Amsterdam and has one brother and six sisters. The family live for a short time in Hilversum but then move back to Amsterdam. They are a religious family: Bep's father is a member of the strict Calvinist Reformed church and her mother is Reformed. All eight children have been baptized and attend Sunday school.

After primary school Bep works several jobs, including as a waitress in a restaurant. Because she wants to advance herself, she takes an evening class in stenography to prepare for a job as an office clerk.

Bep loves dancing and music, and she enjoys going to the cinema to see the latest films. She's a conscientious and considerate young lady who strikes people as rather quiet when she's in a group. But every now and then she can really let her hair down.

Bep comes to work for Otto Frank at Opekta in 1937, and later she also gets to know his family. At 18 she's the youngest employee in the office. She performs a variety of administrative tasks. Later she works as a secretary in the sales department. She shares an office with Miep, who is ten years older. The atmosphere is relaxed and pleasant. At lunchtime they often go for walks together as they eat their sandwiches. Her father, who is unemployed due to health problems, later becomes Opekta's warehouse supervisor.

Bep is the last to be informed about the plans for the Secret Annexe. The others may have had their doubts about involving such a young person in this serious matter (Bep is 22 at the time), since the punishment for helping Jews is severe indeed. When they do entrust Bep with the information, she doesn't let them down: she too agrees to serve as a helper. At that point she cannot fully grasp how much her offer will involve, of course.

> CONTINUED ON P. 131

BEP WITH HER MOTHER
IN AROUND 1939.

PORTRAIT OF THE
VOSKUIJL FAMILY IN
AROUND 1932. BEP IS
SITTING NEXT TO
HER MOTHER.

THREE OPEKTA
EMPLOYEES: PINE,
MIEP AND BEP (RIGHT),
ON THE PRINSEN-
GRACHT, MAY 1941.

THE WEDDING OF BEP AND COR VAN WIJK, 15 MAY 1946. JOHANNA KLEIMAN IS STANDING ON THE FAR LEFT, OTTO FRANK AND CHARLOTTE KALETTA ARE TO THE LEFT OF THE BRIDAL COUPLE. MIEP AND JAN GIES ARE ON THE FAR RIGHT.

BEP AND HER FAMILY,
1960.

LEFT TO RIGHT: BEP'S DAUGHTER ANNE-MARIE, JAN, MIEP AND BEP ON A SUMMER DAY AT

BEP'S HOME ON GALILEIPLANTSOEN IN AMSTERDAM, EARLY SEVENTIES.

OTTO AND FRITZI ON
A VISIT TO BEP, 1978.

BEP, AROUND 1979.

> CONTINUED FROM P. 122

At home, the only one she can share the stress of the responsibility with is her father, whom Otto Frank has also taken into his confidence. No one else knows!

For two long years, she and Miep do the shopping for the occupants of the Secret Annexe. Bep is responsible for the milk and the bread and is also sent to fetch other household necessities, such as cleaning supplies and clothing. When Anne is close to filling up her diary, she writes that she's going to ask Bep to buy her a new one. Bep's sister occasionally sews garments without knowing who they're for, and Bep then brings them to Anne and Margot. Another sister who works for a pharmaceutical firm is sometimes able to provide Bep with medicines. Bep also signs up for correspondence courses in her own name, including stenography for Margot, Peter and Anne, and later Latin for Margot. She tries to make the group as comfortable as possible. For the 1943 Sinterklaas* party, for example, she and Miep dream up all sorts of poems and homemade presents and put them in a large basket as a surprise for the Annexe occupants.

Bep becomes engaged during the war to Bertus Hulsman, but quickly breaks off the engagement. Because her father is becoming increasingly ill and there sometimes isn't enough food at home, she often eats lunch and dinner in the Secret Annexe. She gets on well with Anne, even though Margot is closer to her in age. Sometimes Anne was 'like a sister'[64] to her, Bep later says. They share an interest in movie stars and often gossip together. Anne is delighted with the postcard of the Dutch royal family in Canada that Bep brings her. Bep spends one night in the Secret Annexe* and experiences the tension of life on the other side of the revolving bookcase. She doesn't sleep a wink.

BEP VOSKUIJL

When the Sicherheitsdienst* breaks into the
building on the Prinsengracht on 4 August 1944,
Jo Kleiman quickly sends Bep away. She leaves
the office unhindered. Later she returns, and she
and Miep go up to the Secret Annexe to see if
there are any personal items belonging to their
friends that can be saved. In Edith and Otto's
bedroom they find Anne's red plaid diary lying
on the floor, as well as the loose sheets of paper
and old cashbooks they had given Anne to write
on. Together they pick up all the papers, and
Miep hides them away.

Bep continues to work at Opekta until just after
her marriage to Cor van Wijk in May 1946.
She maintains contact with Otto Frank, even
after his move to Switzerland. Whenever he's
in Amsterdam they go out for lunch, and every
now and then she visits him and his second wife
Fritzi. Otto Frank expresses his gratitude for her
help during the war years by occasionally lending
money to Bep, who always has trouble making
ends meet. Bep and Cor have three sons – Ton,
Cor and Joop – and a daughter, Anne-Marie.
The little girl is named after Anne Frank.
    Bep feels uneasy about the publicity
surrounding Anne Frank and her diary, and she
prefers not to talk about what happened in the
Secret Annexe. But in 1959, when she and Miep
attend a film performance and she is introduced
to Queen Juliana and Princess Beatrix during the
intermission, she admits to feeling 'a little proud
that we were given this great honour'.[65] She stays
in touch with Victor Kugler by mail and visits him
once in Toronto.
    Bep suffers from kidney disease for which she is
hospitalized. She dies there on 6 May 1983, at the
age of 64.

BEP VOSKUIJL

MIEP GIES

AROUND 1935

NAME	**HERMINE GIES-SANTROUSCHITZ**
BORN	**15 FEBRUARY 1909**
	(VIENNA, AUSTRIA)
DIED	**11 JANUARY 2010**
	(HOORN, THE NETHERLANDS)
PSEUDONYM IN	**MIEP VAN SANTEN**
THE DIARY OF	
A YOUNG GIRL	

Anne Frank,
1943[66]

**'Miep has so much to carry
she looks like a pack mule.'**

It's hard to imagine a name more Dutch than Miep Gies, yet few people know that Miep was originally Austrian. She is born in Vienna in 1909 as Hermine Santrouschitz into a poor Catholic family. She has at least one younger sister. During the First World War she becomes undernourished.

Hermine is one of the thousands of Austrian children sent to the Netherlands for three months in 1920 to regain their strength. She ends up in Leiden, where she is placed with the family of Laurens and Johanna Nieuwenburg, who have one daughter and four sons. She stays on and goes to school in Leiden, and her foster parents give her the name Miep. In 1924 the family move to Amsterdam, and the following year they all travel to Vienna. There her real parents and her foster parents decide that Miep is better off in the Netherlands. She grows into a handsome young woman with thick, dark blonde hair and blue eyes.

In Amsterdam Miep completes the three-year ULO* degree and starts looking for work. Her first job is as a typist at Schellekens's Embroidery and Pleating Studios, where she meets Jan Gies. Then in October 1933, wearing a neatly ironed blouse and with her blonde hair done up in a smart chignon, she cycles to Nieuwezijds Voorburgwal to apply for a job at the Opekta company. This bike ride will change her life forever.

At Opekta Miep expects to do office work, but Otto Frank's first assignment is to make jam using Opekta. Miep spends two weeks in the kitchen until she's learned all the tricks of the trade – and she also knows what can go wrong. She's then charged with answering all the customers' questions, by phone and by post. Later Miep is given other tasks as well, such as some of the bookkeeping and typing. She shares the 'front office' on the Prinsengracht with Jo Kleiman and Bep.

Every now and then, she and Jan (whom she is now dating) go to visit Otto Frank at his home on Merwedeplein.

MIEP GIES

> CONTINUED ON P. 142

MIEP AT WORK AT
OPEKTA, 1936.

MIEP (RIGHT) WITH
HER DUTCH FOSTER
MOTHER AND FOSTER
SISTER AND THE WIFE
OF ONE OF HER
FOSTER BROTHERS,
AROUND 1929.

MIEP (SEATED,
SECOND FROM THE
LEFT) VISITING HER
FAMILY IN VIENNA,
AROUND 1930.

ON 16 JULY 1941 MIEP
MARRIES JAN GIES.

OTTO (LEFT) AND MIEP
AND JAN GIES WITH
THEIR SON PAUL, 1950.

MIEP STAYS ACTIVELY
INVOLVED IN THE
WORK OF THE ANNE
FRANK HOUSE UNTIL
AN ADVANCED AGE,
AND SHE REGULARLY
TAKES VISITORS ON
TOURS; THIS IS IN
THE NINETIES.

MIEP IN 1992:
INTERVIEWS NO
LONGER BOTHER HER.

> CONTINUED FROM P. 134

In the early summer of 1941, Jan and Miep
– who has been living with her foster parents
in the Rivierenbuurt up until now – finally find
a home: they can rent a couple of rooms from
a woman in Hunzestraat. They'll be able to marry
as soon as Jan is divorced from his first wife.
Finally the big day comes on 16 July 1941. In her
free time Miep Gies enjoys playing cards with
her friends, and she also takes dancing lessons.
She and Jan share a love of Mozart's music.

On Sunday evening, 5 July 1942, Hermann van
Pels comes to warn Miep and Jan that the Frank
family are going into hiding earlier than expected.
Miep and Jan go to Merwedeplein to take away
as many of the Frank family's belongings as they
can, concealing them under their coats. The
next morning, Miep cycles with Margot to the
Prinsengracht in order to hide her in the Secret
Annexe* before the other personnel arrive.
The rest of the family follow later.

For two years, Miep and Bep do the shopping
for the Annexe occupants: Miep gets the meat
from the trustworthy butcher whom she came
to know through Hermann van Pels; for the
vegetables she tries to go to a different shop every
time. The responsibility sometimes weighs heavy
on her shoulders, but she does her best to remain
cheerful for the sake of the group. Every Saturday
she also brings five library books along, which the
Annexe occupants eagerly anticipate. 'Ordinary
people don't know how much books can mean
to someone who's cooped up,' Anne writes.[67]
Each book is devoured by several of them.

It's through Miep that Fritz Pfeffer becomes
the eighth to go into hiding. His arrival brings
with it an extra job: now Miep will meet regularly
with Fritz's girlfriend Charlotte Kaletta to
exchange letters and packages with her. It's a
dangerous business, but she's glad to do it for
Dr Pfeffer: after all, he's gone into hiding without
any family and he needs the contact.

In hiding
—
**Pack mule
and carrier
pigeon**

MIEP GIES

Miep and Jan are treated to a dinner in the Secret Annexe to celebrate their first wedding anniversary. Auguste van Pels cooks a delicious meal and Anne types the menu. Since the spring of 1943, Miep and Jan have also been hiding a young man in their own home, Kuno van der Horst, who stays with them for quite some time. They live under constant tension. The occupants of the Secret Annexe know nothing about this.

During the raid of 4 August 1944 Miep is threatened with a pistol and told to stay seated. Later SD* officer Karl Joseph Silberbauer comes in. It emerges that he too is from Vienna, just like Miep. This surprises Silberbauer; he does not arrest her, even though he suspects her of being an accessory. Later on, when she and Bep go up to the Secret Annexe to view the shambles left behind, they find Anne's diaries. Miep keeps them in her desk drawer.

She continues to work as best she can. The liberation of 5 May 1945 leaves her with mixed feelings: the country is free, and she knows that Kuno has safely made it through the war, but she has no idea what has become of the group of eight. Then on 3 June 1945 Otto suddenly appears on the Gies's doorstep on 3 June 1945. He knows that Edith has died. Miep and Jan offer him hospitality in their home. He will end up spending seven years with them. After several weeks, when it becomes clear that Anne and Margot both died in Bergen-Belsen, Miep gives all Anne's writings to Otto Frank.

In 1950, when their only child Paul is born, Miep stops working. She regards caring for three men at home – Jan, Otto and little Paul – as a full-time job.

She still plays canasta every week, now with Charlotte Kaletta and other friends, including Jo Kleiman and his wife. After Otto Frank leaves for Switzerland she keeps in touch with him, discussing personal matters as well as the publications, films and plays having to do with the diary and the Secret Annexe.

In 1959, when the Dutch World Service invites her to give a radio interview, she writes to Otto: 'it will be a snap for me, I no longer dread these kinds of things'.[68] After Otto Frank dies in 1980, Miep is regarded as something of a representative of the Secret Annexe occupants, and she corresponds with people from all over the world.

Every year on 4 August, the day of the betrayal, Miep and Jan close their curtains and take their telephone off the hook. This is how they commemorate the tragedy of the Secret Annexe and their departed friends.

Ten years after Jan's death, Miep moves to Hoorn, where her son Paul lives. She continues to be involved in the activities of the Anne Frank House up to the very last. In 2010 she dies at the impressive age of 100.

JAN GIES

1940

NAME	————————————	JAN AUGUSTUS GIES
BORN	————————————	18 AUGUST 1905
		(AMSTERDAM, THE NETHERLANDS)
DIED	————————————	26 JANUARY 1993
		(AMSTERDAM, THE NETHERLANDS)
PSEUDONYM IN	————————————	HENK VAN SANTEN
THE DIARY OF		
A YOUNG GIRL		

Jan Gies, on his resistance activities, 1989[69] ———————————— 'You suppress it [...]. Even in your other life you suppress it. Actually you live two lives.'

JAN GIES

Jan Gies is an Amsterdammer, born and bred. He is the youngest in a family of five children. Nothing is known of his school years or of any further training he may have had. In 1928 Jan marries Maria Margaretha Geertruida Netten, from whom he is officially divorced in 1940, although he has been living alone in a boarding house since 1936. He becomes close friends with Jo and Wim Bunjes, the daughter and son-in-law of his landlord and landlady. In the early thirties he meets Miep Santrouschitz at Schellekens's Embroidery and Pleating Studios, where Jan works as a bookkeeper. He and Miep occasionally play cards with Wim and Jo Bunjes. They also enjoy poking around at flea markets. He is a tall man with round glasses, dark wavy hair that he combs back, and a friendly, modest personality. He is not religious.

In around 1936, Miep introduces Jan to Otto Frank and his family. As the years pass, a relationship of trust also develops with Otto. In around 1939 Jan is given a job at the Municipal Bureau for Social Affairs in the Department of Social Support. He continues his work as a civil servant throughout the war. In 1941, at Otto Frank's request, Jan and Victor Kugler set up the firm Gies & Co, and Jan is appointed director of the company.

Through his job, Jan Gies becomes involved in the resistance, enabling him to obtain ration coupons* for the occupants of the Secret Annexe on a regular basis. His work involves cycling throughout the city to deliver mail and packages to various addresses, so he can easily carry illegal items without being spotted. He is also probably involved in finding hiding places for Jews and others who have been called up for the *Arbeitseinsatz**. His exact activities are not known because he never discussed them with anyone, not even later with Miep or his son Paul.

> CONTINUED ON P. 151

JAN,
10 NOVEMBER 1953.

SCHELLEKENS'S
EMBROIDERY AND
PLEATING STUDIOS,
WHERE JAN AND
MIEP GET TO KNOW
EACH OTHER.

MIEP AND JAN WITH
THEIR GUESTS AT THE
DOOR OF 263 PRINSEN-
GRACHT ON THEIR
WEDDING DAY. ANNE
FRANK IS ON THE FAR
RIGHT. THIS IS THE ONLY
KNOWN POSED GROUP
PHOTO FROM THAT DAY,
16 JULY 1941.

JAN, MIEP AND THEIR
SON PAUL VISITING
OTTO AND FRITZI IN
SWITZERLAND,
EARLY SIXTIES.

AFTER THE WAR THE
HELPERS STAY IN
TOUCH. BACK ROW:
JAN AND VICTOR.

FRONT ROW: MIEP, BEP,
COR VAN WIJK AND
LOES KUGLER.
AROUND 1973.

> CONTINUED FROM P. 146

On 16 July 1941, Jan – dressed in a handsome grey suit – makes his way to the town hall with his new bride, where Miep's foster parents, Otto and Anne Frank, Hermann and Auguste van Pels and a few other friends are waiting for them. During the ceremony, Jan places the gold wedding ring on Miep's finger. They only have enough money for one ring, so he has to wait for better times to purchase his own.

In hiding
—
Responsibility for ration coupons

Jan Gies is deeply involved in the Secret Annexe* plans. During the first week he and Miep make several trips to the Annexe, carrying the Frank family's personal belongings. He provides the ration coupons, which Miep and Bep use to buy food. He also comes to visit almost every day. He eats lunch with Miep in the office and then goes upstairs. He always tries to obtain cigarettes for Hermann van Pels, but the others look forward to his visits as well. Jan frequently joins them in the Secret Annexe at lunchtime and tells them all the latest news, while Mouschi jumps on his lap. They hang on his every word.

After discovery
—
'Prince consort'

On 4 August 1944 Jan comes to have lunch once again on the Prinsengracht, but Miep is able to warn him just in time: she hands him the illegal ration coupons* and his lunch with the words, 'It's wrong here'.[70] He watches from the other side of the canal as the Secret Annexe occupants, along with Kleiman and Kugler, are taken away. To be on the safe side, Miep and Jan tell the young man hiding in their home that he'll have to look for another address. Kuno van der Horst goes back to his mother in Hilversum.

After liberation, Otto Frank is the only one of the group to return, and he moves in with Jan and Miep. On 13 July 1950, when Miep gives birth to a healthy son, Paul Augustus, Jan is over the moon: they had stopped hoping for a child.

JAN GIES

Their friendship with the Bunjes family continues after the war, as do their card-playing evenings. In all the publicity around the diary, the Secret Annexe and the helpers, Jan prefers to take a back seat. He's only too glad to let Miep do the talking. He faithfully accompanies her everywhere, calling himself 'the prince consort'. In 1978 they even go to Japan, where they have been invited to open an exhibition on Anne Frank.

Jan dies in 1993; he is 87 years old.

JAN GIES

OTHERS IN AND AROUND 263 PRINSENGRACHT

Anne Frank, 1944[71]

'Mr Van Hoeven [sic] obviously suspects we're here, because he always delivers the potatoes at lunchtime. A decent chap!'

Johannes Voskuijl (in *The Diary of a Young Girl* he's given the pseudonym Mr Vossen) works briefly as a furniture salesman and later as a bookkeeper for various companies and private individuals. In around 1935 his activities are greatly restricted due to illness (stomach cancer). He sits at home and worries because he has a large family to support. His oldest daughter, Bep, takes a job at Opekta in 1937, and in 1941 Otto Frank hires the sickly Johannes as warehouse supervisor. Otto entrusts both of them with his plans for going into hiding.

Johannes Voskuil constructs the revolving bookcase hiding the entrance to the Secret Annexe*. Several of the presents that the Annexe occupants receive from the helpers for the 1942 Sinterklaas* party are made by him: an ashtray for Hermann van Pels, a picture frame for Fritz Pfeffer and a pair of bookends for Otto Frank.

In the warehouse, he and the workers are responsible for provisioning and for maintaining the spice mill and the grinding machines. They also make, weigh and pack the herb mixtures. Johannes keeps an eye on things, and every morning he carries out the rubbish that Peter puts in the warehouse the night before. In 1943 his illness takes a turn for the worse and he can no longer work, although he does come for occasional visits. Shortly after the war, on 27 November 1945, Johannes Voskuijl passes away.

Willem van Maaren succeeds Johannes Voskuijl as warehouse supervisor in the spring of 1943. With his arrival, the sense of security that the group had with Johannes Voskuijl is gone. According to Anne, Van Maaren is 'getting suspicious about the Annexe'[72], and sometimes he even sets traps in the warehouse: he places a pencil on end on the table, for instance, so he can see whether someone has come in after closing time. Obviously he suspects that something is going on in the Secret Annexe.

JOHANNES VOSKUIJL,
AROUND 1932.

WILLEM VAN MAAREN,
PROBABLY 1963.

JOHANNES JACOBUS
DE KOK, DATE
UNKNOWN.

HENDRIK PIETER
DAATZELAAR,
DATE UNKNOWN.

MARTIN BROUWER,
DATE UNKNOWN.

JOHN BROKS, 1941.

HENDRIK VAN HOEVE
WITH HIS WIFE AND
SON, 1941.

HENDRIK VAN HOEVE'S
GREENGROCER'S SHOP
AT 58 LELIEGRACHT,
AROUND 1940. HIS
WIFE RIEK IS STANDING
IN THE DOORWAY.

There are also two temporary warehouse workers employed during the hiding period: Lammert Hartog and Johannes Jacobus de Kok. The latter is an acrobat and a sailor, among other things. It later emerges that he and Van Maaren were also involved in several thefts at Opekta and Gies & Co.

Cats

In around 1940, 263 Prinsengracht becomes home to two cats who are meant to keep the building free of rodents. When the group moves in to the Secret Annexe, only Boche is left – the 'warehouse and office cat', as Anne calls him.[73] Anne has already had to say good-bye to her own black cat, Moortje, who has found a new home with the neighbours on Merwedeplein. She misses Moortje 'every minute of the day'.[74] The black cat Mouschi that Peter brings to the Secret Annexe is little consolation at first because Anne is rather afraid of him. Later they get used to each other. Mouschi sometimes stretches himself out across one of Anne's knees and one of Margot's, and there he sleeps.

The cats also have their drawbacks, as the occupants discover. When there's no more peat available for his litter box up in the loft, Mouschi pees next to the box into a pile of wood shavings. The pee drips down between the floor boards and, 'as luck would have it, landed in and next to the potato barrel'.[75]

In late April 1944, Boche disappears without a trace, and Anne reports that Peter is deeply distressed. Warehouse cat Boche is followed by 't Scharminkeltje, or little bag of bones. As the name suggests, he's a skinny beast who can't stand pepper and is not housebroken. So he doesn't last long. During the arrest Mouschi runs off, but after a couple of days he suddenly comes strolling back into the office. From then on, Miep takes care of him and he becomes the new office cat.

The chemist and the neighbours

Before the Secret Annexe becomes a hiding place, the second floor of the *achterhuis* is used by Arthur Lewinsohn, a Jewish chemist and pharmacist who does chemical testing for both companies. During the hiding period he occasionally uses the company kitchen on the first floor for his work. Because Lewinsohn knows the building from top to bottom, the group are forced to remain completely silent.

On workdays, the Annexe occupants, who live on the second and third floors of the thin-walled *achterhuis*, have to be as quiet as mice starting at half past eight in the morning, because the warehouse workers on the ground floor must never suspect that people are hiding in the building. They also have to make sure that the neighbours – Keg to the left (coffee and tea merchants) and Elhoek to the right (furniture maker and upholsterer) – don't notice anything. There are Jews in hiding all over Amsterdam, some of them nearby in just this kind of *achterhuis*.

Sales representatives

Sales representatives are regular visitors to the office part of the building. They discuss the purchasing and sale of goods with Kugler and Kleiman. Sales reps Hendrik Pieter Daatzelaar and Martin Brouwer drop in at Gies & Co at least once a week. In 1944, when the two are picked up for dealing in illegal ration coupons*, it's a heavy blow for the group in hiding: apparently these sales reps also delivered extra coupons to Gies & Co, which were then used for the occupants of the Annexe.

In the summer of 1944, the office receives an enormous shipment of strawberries via John Broks and his wife Ans Broks-Bossen, who have been procuring orders for Opekta for years. The Annexe occupants immediately convert the strawberries into jam and compote – with the help of Opekta, of course!

Sometimes there are important discussions, such as the time sales reps arrive from Germany. Otto wants to be there so badly that he and Margot lie with their ears pressed to the floor boards in order to follow the conversation below.

In the afternoon Anne takes over because her father is absolutely exhausted, but she falls asleep during the boring discussions.

Deliverymen: the butcher, the baker and the greengrocer

With eight mouths to feed, Bep and Miep have a lot of shopping to do. The greengrocer on the Leliegracht, Hendrik van Hoeve (which is where Miep regularly shops), brings the heavy sacks of potatoes to the Prinsengracht himself. He does this during his lunch break, so the warehouse workers don't know anything about it. Van Hoeve himself is also hiding Jews at home, and one day he is arrested. After the war, Otto Frank looks the greengrocer up: it seems he survived four concentration camps.

The bread for the occupants of the Annexe is delivered twice or three times a week by Simons the baker. In exchange for lactose, he delivers unrationed bread: bread that can be bought for cash alone, without the need for ration coupons. Before going into hiding, Hermann van Pels works out an agreement with a friendly butcher so that Miep will be able to get her meat there. The milk is delivered every day and brought upstairs by Bep. Thus the helpers are always able to obtain enough food, although the portions become smaller and smaller and of increasingly inferior quality.

There are also cleaning people who occasionally work in the office; their identity is not known. At one point a plumber and a carpenter enter the building to move some pipes. The helpers must be constantly alert to who is coming and going.

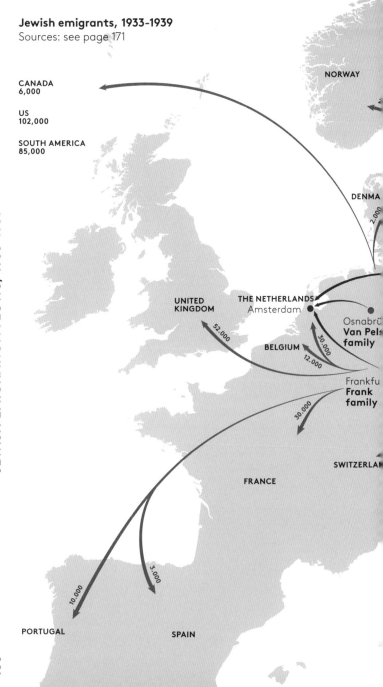

Jewish emigrants, 1933-1939
Sources: see page 171

CANADA
6,000

US
102,000

SOUTH AMERICA
85,000

JEWISH EMIGRATION FLOWS, 1933-1939

NORWAY

DENMA

2.000

UNITED
KINGDOM

THE NETHERLANDS
Amsterdam

Osnabrü
Van Pel
family

52.000

BELGIUM

30.000

12.000

Frankfu
Frank
family

30.000

SWITZERLA

FRANCE

10.000

3.000

PORTUGAL

SPAIN

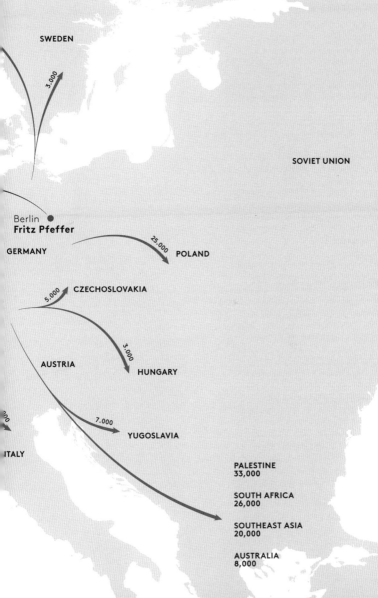

SWEDEN

3.000

SOVIET UNION

Berlin
Fritz Pfeffer

GERMANY

25.000

POLAND

5.000 CZECHOSLOVAKIA

3.000

AUSTRIA

HUNGARY

7.000

200

YUGOSLAVIA

ITALY

PALESTINE
33,000

SOUTH AFRICA
26,000

SOUTHEAST ASIA
20,000

AUSTRALIA
8,000

JEWISH EMIGRATION FLOWS, 1933-1939

Amersfoort

Johannes Kleiman is interned in Camp Amersfoort. On 18 September 1944 he is released.
Victor Kugler is imprisoned in Camp Amersfoort for quite some time (and later in Zwolle and Wageningen). In March 1945 he is put on a march to Germany for forced labour but succeeds in escaping.

Auschwitz and Auschwitz-Birkenau*

Hermann van Pels is killed in Auschwitz, probably in October/November 1944.
Edith Frank dies in Auschwitz-Birkenau on 6 January 1945.
Otto Frank is freed from Auschwitz on 27 January 1945.

Bergen-Belsen

In late October or early November 1944, Anne and Margot are deported from Auschwitz to Bergen-Belsen (Auguste van Pels is probably on the same transport). Both girls die in March 1945.

Mauthausen

When Auschwitz is cleared in late January 1945, Peter van Pels is put on a 'death march'. The march ends in Mauthausen. Peter van Pels dies there, probably in the second half of April 1945.

Neuengamme

In October 1944, Fritz Pfeffer is moved from Auschwitz to Neuengamme. He dies there in December 1944.

Raguhn (Buchenwald)

In late October or early November 1944 Auguste van Pels is deported from Auschwitz to Bergen-Belsen, and in February 1945 she is moved to Raguhn (a satellite camp of Buchenwald). She dies in April 1945 during a transport from Raguhn to Theresienstadt.

Westerbork

In August 1944 the eight Secret Annexe occupants are deported to Westerbork, and in early September from there to Auschwitz.

Neuengamm

Westerbork ●

Bergen
Belsen

Amsterdam ●
●

Amersfoort

Brussels ●

Luxembourg ●

Bern ●

TIMELINE

Anne Frank,
11 april 1944[76]

———————

'One day this terrible war will
be over. The time will come
when we'll be people again
and not just Jews!'

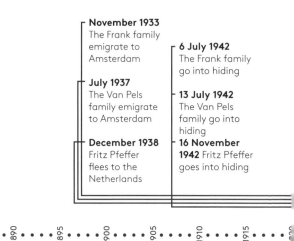

November 1933
The Frank family emigrate to Amsterdam

July 1937
The Van Pels family emigrate to Amsterdam

December 1938
Fritz Pfeffer flees to the Netherlands

6 July 1942
The Frank family go into hiding

13 July 1942
The Van Pels family go into hiding

16 November 1942 Fritz Pfeffer goes into hiding

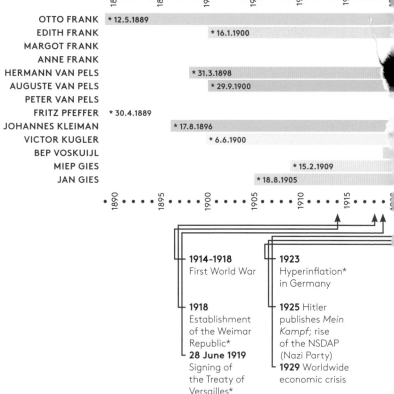

	1890	1895	1900	1905	1910	1915
OTTO FRANK	* 12.5.1889					
EDITH FRANK			* 16.1.1900			
MARGOT FRANK						
ANNE FRANK						
HERMANN VAN PELS			* 31.3.1898			
AUGUSTE VAN PELS			* 29.9.1900			
PETER VAN PELS						
FRITZ PFEFFER	* 30.4.1889					
JOHANNES KLEIMAN		* 17.8.1896				
VICTOR KUGLER			* 6.6.1900			
BEP VOSKUIJL						
MIEP GIES					* 15.2.1909	
JAN GIES				* 18.8.1905		

1914–1918
First World War

1918
Establishment of the Weimar Republic*

28 June 1919
Signing of the Treaty of Versailles*

1923
Hyperinflation* in Germany

1925 Hitler publishes *Mein Kampf*; rise of the NSDAP (Nazi Party)

1929 Worldwide economic crisis

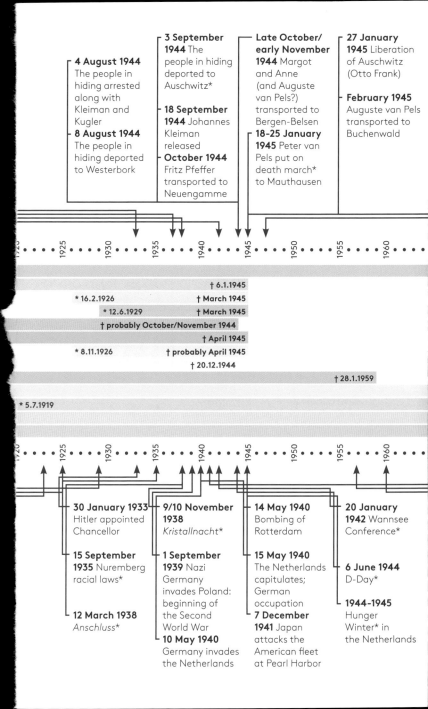

4 August 1944 The people in hiding arrested along with Kleiman and Kugler

8 August 1944 The people in hiding deported to Westerbork

3 September 1944 The people in hiding deported to Auschwitz*

18 September 1944 Johannes Kleiman released

October 1944 Fritz Pfeffer transported to Neuengamme

Late October/ early November 1944 Margot and Anne (and Auguste van Pels?) transported to Bergen-Belsen

18-25 January 1945 Peter van Pels put on death march* to Mauthausen

27 January 1945 Liberation of Auschwitz (Otto Frank)

February 1945 Auguste van Pels transported to Buchenwald

† 6.1.1945

* 16.2.1926   † March 1945

* 12.6.1929   † March 1945

† probably October/November 1944

† April 1945

* 8.11.1926   † probably April 1945

† 20.12.1944

† 28.1.1959

* 5.7.1919

30 January 1933 Hitler appointed Chancellor

15 September 1935 Nuremberg racial laws*

12 March 1938 *Anschluss**

9/10 November 1938 *Kristallnacht**

1 September 1939 Nazi Germany invades Poland: beginning of the Second World War

10 May 1940 Germany invades the Netherlands

14 May 1940 Bombing of Rotterdam

15 May 1940 The Netherlands capitulates; German occupation

7 December 1941 Japan attacks the American fleet at Pearl Harbor

20 January 1942 Wannsee Conference*

6 June 1944 D-Day*

1944-1945 Hunger Winter* in the Netherlands

● Copenhagen

● Berlin
Warsaw ●

Raguhn
●
Buchenwald
●
Theresien-
● **stadt**
Prague ●
● **Auschwitz**

●   ● Vienna
Mauthausen
Budapest ●

Around 24 March 1945
Victor Kugler escapes imprisonment

April 1945
Auguste van Pels transported to Theresienstadt, killed along the way

3 June 1945
Otto Frank returns to Amsterdam

25 June 1947
Publication of *Het Achterhuis* by Anne Frank

1970 • • • • 1975 • • • • 1980 • • • • 1985 • • • • 1990 • • • • 1995 • • • • 2000 • • • • 2005 • • • • 2010

† 19.8.1980

† 14.12.1981

† 6.5.1983

† 11.1.2010

† 26.1.1993

1970 • • • • 1975 • • • • 1980 • • • • 1985 • • • • 1990 • • • • 1995 • • • • 2000 • • • • 2005 • • • • 2010

30 April 1945
Hitler commits suicide

5 May 1945
Liberation of the Netherlands

8 May 1945
Germany surrenders

3 May 1957
Founding of the Anne Frank House (foundation)

3 May 1960
Opening of the Anne Frank House (museum)

ACHTERHUIS (AND VOORHUIS)

In the 17th century, known as the Golden Age, the canals of Amsterdam were highly sought-after locations for well-to-do businessmen, since all goods were transported by water. As a result, many deep, narrow buildings were constructed on the canals. In later centuries, a growing population made it necessary to build additions onto the backs of the buildings. Such an addition was called an *achterhuis* in Dutch.

Please note: In this book, the back section is called the Secret Annexe when the hiding place is being referred to, which is how *achterhuis* is translated in the English edition of Anne's diary. When reference is made to the entire back part of the building, the architectural term *achterhuis* is used.

ANSCHLUSS

On 12 March 1938, Austria was occupied and annexed by the Nazis. This *Anschluss* was Hitler's first step towards a greater German Reich that would include all German-speaking peoples.

ARBEITSEINSATZ

Initially a voluntary employment scheme, after 1940 it was mainly forced labour involving workers from the Nazi occupied territories and was used to benefit the German war industry.

ARYANIZATION

When a company was Aryanized, it meant that the Jewish owners, shareholders, etc., had been dispossessed. The term is taken from the word 'Aryan', the name given to the so-called superior Germanic race in Nazi ideology.

ASSIGNEE WITH POWER OF ATTORNEY

Someone authorized to carry out certain activities in the name of the company without being its director or owner.

AUSCHWITZ (AUSCHWITZ I, AUSCHWITZ-BIRKENAU)

The Auschwitz extermination and concentration camp (German name for the nearby Polish town of Oświęcim) consisted of several parts: the Auschwitz *Stammlager* (Auschwitz I), Auschwitz-Birkenau (Auschwitz II), Auschwitz-Monowitz (Auschwitz III) and several subcamps or so-called 'outside commandos'.

AUSSENLAGER

A satellite camp of a 'main' concentration camp; most camps had several *Aussenlager*.

D-DAY

On 6 June 1944, known as D-Day, Allied troops (American, British, Canadian and a number of other nationalities) landed on the coast of Normandy, France, thus breaking through the Western front and beginning the advance through the German lines.

DAS REICH

Das Reich was a weekly newspaper distributed by the NSDAP (Nazi Party) between 1940 and 1945, mainly in Nazi Germany but also in a few occupied countries such as the Netherlands.

DEATH MARCH

At the end of the war, with the advance of the Soviet armies in the east, the Nazis evacuated the concentration camps in an attempt to eradicate all traces of their atrocities. Large groups of prisoners were forced to march west across enormous distances. These were later called death marches because of the vast numbers of victims that resulted.

ENDLÖSUNG

Literally 'final solution', a euphemism for the Nazis' plan to exterminate the entire Jewish population of Europe.

HAAGSCHE POST

The *Haagsche Post* was a popular Dutch news magazine founded in 1914 by the Jewish S.F. van Oss. During the war the German occupiers took it over, and as a result it was less politically explicit and dealt mainly with other issues.

HOLOCAUST

The Holocaust was the systematic persecution and murder of approximately six million European Jews by the Nazis and their confederates before and during the Second World War.

HUNGER WINTER

During the severe winter of 1944-1945 there was a serious scarcity of food and fuel in the western provinces of the Netherlands. With liberation in sight, 20,000 lives were lost.

HYPERINFLATION

Inflation occurring at an extremely high rate. The German economy was struck by hyperinflation in 1922-1923 when, staggering under the reparations that had been imposed after the First World War, Germany began printing extra money to keep up with day-to-day expenses. At the same time the loans continued to mount. The money shrank in value so rapidly that between December 1921 and November 1923 the price of a kilo of bread skyrocketed from 4 to 201 billion German marks.

JEHOVAH'S WITNESSES

Jehovah's Witnesses are members of a religious group related to Protestantism that was founded in the late 19th century. They were fanatically persecuted by the Nazis on account of their fundamental belief in allegiance to God alone and their refusal to recognize the authority of any state or political party.

JEWISH STAR

On 3 May 1942, the Nazis required all the Jews of the Netherlands six years old and older to wear a Jewish star. This six-pointed star, drawn in black, was made of yellow cotton and bore the word 'Jew'. It was to be sewn onto the clothing at breast height on the left side and was to be clearly visible. The design was derived from the Star of David, a symbol of Judaism.

KRÄTZEBLOCK

Because of all the vermin, many prisoners in the concentration camps contracted scabies or other skin diseases. Due to the danger of contagion, prisoners with such skin disorders were housed in isolated barracks known as the *Krätzeblock* or 'scabies barracks'.

KRISTALLNACHT

Kristallnacht was an explosion of anti-Jewish hatred organized by the Nazis that took place on the night of 9-10 November 1938. Throughout Germany, violent attacks were carried out on Jews and Jewish homes, shops, synagogues, schools, hospitals and cemeteries. More than a hundred Jews were murdered and more than 30,000 Jewish men were arrested and sent to prisons and concentration camps. The incident is called *Kristallnacht* because of the many broken windows that resulted.

MONTESSORI SCHOOLS

An educational method developed by the Italian doctor and educator Maria Montessori (1870-1952), based on the idea that each child has a natural need for self-development. The method caters to this need and provides the pupil with specially designed materials at just the right moment.

MULO OR ULO

(Meer) Uitgebreid Lager Onderwijs – Advanced Elementary Education – was a type of Dutch secondary school. It offered a standard curriculum (no optional courses). In 1968 it was replaced by the MAVO.

NUREMBERG RACIAL LAWS
On 15 September 1935, Hitler issued the Nuremberg racial laws. These laws determined who was and who was not Jewish, among other things. The civil rights of Jews were restricted and Jews were not permitted to marry or have sexual relations with non-Jews.

PULS, PULSEN
Abraham Puls of Amsterdam had been a member of the National Socialist Movement in the Netherlands (NSB, a Dutch fascist party) since 1934. His removal company acquired a bad reputation when, by order of the German occupiers, it began clearing the homes of Jews who had been deported or gone into hiding and sending all useful materials to Germany. This even gave rise to a new Dutch verb: *pulsen*.

RATION REGISTRATION CARDS AND RATION COUPONS
As the threat of war increased in the late thirties, the Dutch government introduced a rationing system in order to guarantee an adequate food supply. This system worked by means of ration registration cards and ration coupons. The issuing of the ration registration card was linked to the municipal register. The registration card had to be picked up in person, but the coupons could also be picked up by others. With a coupon you could buy a fixed amount of food or other products. Anyone not listed in the municipal register was not issued a registration card and therefore received no ration coupons. The rationing system was continued during the occupation. It was also frequently sabotaged, and a lively trade was conducted in illegal and counterfeit ration coupons.

REPARATIONS
After the First World War, Germany was singled out as the party chiefly responsible for the Allies' war damages. As the losing party, it was made to pay exorbitant amounts of money in compensation to all the other parties.

ROMA AND SINTI
Popularly known as gypsies (a name they regard as offensive): originally nomadic peoples, probably from India, who began settling in Europe in the 15th century. The Roma, to which the Sinti belong, have a long history of repression in Europe and were fanatically persecuted, deported and murdered under the Nazi regime.

SECRET ANNEXE
See *achterhuis*.

SICHERHEITSDIENST (SD)
The Sicherheitsdienst was originally the intelligence service of the NSDAP, the German Nazi party, but it soon developed into the state intelligence service for all of Nazi Germany. Regional divisions of the Sicherheitsdienst were also established in the occupied areas.

SINTERKLAAS
Sinterklaas, or Saint Nicholas, is the central figure in a popular celebration of the same name that takes place in the Netherlands on 5 December. Children place their shoes near the fireplace and, according to tradition, Sinterklaas's helper, Black Pete, fills them with presents and sweets. Adults celebrate the holiday by giving each other original surprises or presents accompanied by poems they write themselves.

SINTI
see Roma

TREATY OF VERSAILLES
Having been singled out as the main guilty party in the First World War, Germany was more or less forced

by the Allies to accept the exacting terms of the Treaty of Versailles. The treaty required Germany to part with all of its colonies and several other territories and to pay enormous reparations to the Allies in compensation for the war damages they had suffered.

ULO
see MULO

WANNSEE CONFERENCE
A secret meeting of senior Nazi officials held on 20 January 1942 at Villa Marlier on the Wannsee in Berlin. Here the systematic implementation of the *Endlösung** was discussed.

WEIMAR REPUBLIC
This German republic, established in 1918 after the First World War, was the successor to the German Empire. When Hitler was appointed chancellor in 1933 he suspended the constitution, and within one year he had seized total power. This takeover marked the end of the democratic Weimar Republic and the beginning of Nazi dictatorship.

THE FOLLOWING SOURCES WERE USED IN THIS BOOK:

Material from the knowledge centre and documents from the Anne Frank Collection and the Anne Frank House.

Anne Frank House (ed.)
Anne Frank House: A Museum with a Story, Amsterdam: Anne Frank House, 1999.

Bade, Klaus J. (ed.)
The Encyclopedia of Migration and Minorities in Europe from the 17th Century to the Present, Cambridge: Cambridge University Press, 2011.

Frank, Anne
The Diary of a Young Girl, London: Penguin Books, 1997.

Frank, Anne
The Diary of Anne Frank: The Critical Edition, prepared by the Netherlands State Institute for War Documentation; introduced by Harry Paape, Gerrold van der Stroom and David Bernouw; edited by David Barnouw and Gerrold van der Stroom; New York: Doubleday, 1989.

Gies, Miep & Alison Leslie Gold
Anne Frank Remembered: the Story of the Woman Who Helped to Hide the Frank Family, New York: Simon & Schuster, 1987.

Gilbert, Martin
Atlas of the Holocaust, Cornwall: William Morrow & Company, 1993.

Gold, Alison Leslie
Memories of Anne Frank: Reflections of a Childhood Friend, New York: Scholastic Press, 1997.

Lans, Jos van der and Herman Vuijsje
Het Anne Frank Huis: Een biografie [The Anne Frank House: A Biography], Amsterdam: Boom, 2010.

Ledden, Piet van & Menno Metselaar (eds.)
Anne's wereld [Anne's World], Amsterdam: Anne Frank House, 2010.

Müller, Melissa
Anne Frank: The Biography, New York: Metropolitan Books, 1998.

Schnabel, Ernst
Anne Frank: A Portrait in Courage, New York: Harcourt, Brace and Company 1958.

SOURCES QUOTED

Frank, Anne
The Diary of a Young Girl, **London: Penguin Books, 1997.**
Citation numbers 15 (5 August 1943), **17** (3 May 1944), **18** (13 December 1942), **19** (4 March 1943), **20** (19 January 1944), **21** (31 March 1944), **29** (16 May 1944), **31** (5 November 1942 en 12 January 1944), **32** (21 August 1942), **33** (20 March 1944), **35** (19 March 1943), **37** (23 July 1943), **38** (29 October 1943), **41** (9 August 1943), **48** (13 June 1944), **50** (9 August 1943), **53** (10 September 1943), **55** (3 August 1943), **66** (11 July 1943), **67** (11 July 1943), **71** (11 April 1944), **72** (16 September 1943), **73** (12 March 1943), **74** (12 July 1942), **75** (10 May 1944), **76** (11 April 1944).

Frank, Anne
*The Diary of Anne Frank:
The Critical Edition*, **New York: Doubleday, 1989**
Citation number 16 (5 August 1943).

Gies, Miep & Alison Leslie Gold
Anne Frank Remembered: the Story of the Woman Who Helped to Hide the Frank Family, **New York: Simon & Schuster, 1987.**
Citation numbers 5 (p. 114), **22** (p. 114-115), **42** (p. 47), **43** (p. 47), **44** (p. 109), **46** (pp. 173-174), **54** (p. 55), **70** (p. 187).

Gold, Alison Leslie
*Memories of Anne Frank:
Reflections of a Childhood Friend*, **New York: Scholastic Press, 1997**
Citatation number 40 (p. 104).

Schnabel, Ernst
Anne Frank: A Portrait in Courage, **New York: Harcourt, Brace and Company, 1958**
Citation numbers 39 (p. 120), **57** (p. 118), **64** (p. 86).

Archive of the Anne Frank House (AFS):
Citation numbers 1 Johannes Kleiman in a radio interview about Otto Frank, 12 June 1957; **2** AFS interview with Toos-Buiteman-Kupers, 23 October 2009, 12a; **3** AFS interview with Barbara Rodbell-Ledermann, 1 and 2 October 2008, 1b; **4** AFS interview with Barbara Rodbell-Ledermann, 1 and 2 October 2008, 1a; **6** AFS interview with Bertel Freund-Hess, 22 March 1997; **7** AFS interview with Eva Meyer, 20 February 2010, 18a; **8** Interview with Werner Pfeffer conducted by Jon Blair, in preparation for the film *Anne Frank Remembered*, 1995, p. 1; **10** Manuscript of Eda Shapiro (ed.), *Victor Kugler: The Man Who Hid Anne Frank*, 1996; **11** AFS interview with Cor van Wijk, 2 February 2007; **12** AFS interview with Jacqueline Sanders-van Maarsen, 30 September 2009, 11c; **13** AFS interview with Eva Geiringer-Schloss, 12 and 13 November 2008, 2k; **14** AFS interview with Cor van Wijk, 2 February 2007; **25** Letter from Alice Frank to Otto Frank, 19 June 1945; **26** Letter from Edith Frank to Gertrud Naumann, 22 December 1937; **27** Letter from Edith Frank to Gertrud Naumann, 23 December 1933; **28** Letter from Edith Frank to Hedda Eisenstedt, 24 December 1937; **34** Latin Course, lesson 9, with corrections by A.C. Nielson, Archive of the Anne Frank House, on loan from the Netherlands Institute for War Documentation; **36** Johannes Kleiman in a letter to S. Braaksma-Van Heerikhuizen, 27 February 1953; **47** AFS interview with Hannah Pick-Goslar, 6 May 2009, 8e; **49** AFS interview with Ralph Jacobson, 14 March 1996; **52** AFS interview with Alfred Sand, 29 August 1995; **56** Postcard from Johannes Kleiman to Erich Elias, dated 6 September 1943; **58** Inscription in the book *Weerklank van Anne Frank*, which Otto Frank sent Victor Kugler, 26 April 1970; **59**, **60**, **61**, Manuscript of Eda Shapiro (ed.) *Victor Kugler: The Man Who Hid*

Anne Frank, 1996; **63** Letter from Bep Voskuijl to Otto Frank, 4 September 1957; **65** Letter from Bep Voskuijl to Victor Kugler, 1 June 1959; **68** Letter from Miep Gies to Otto and Fritzi Frank, 21 April 1959; **69** Interview with Miep and Jan Gies, 20 December 1989.

Otto Frank archive:
Citation numbers 9 Letter from Victor Kugler to Otto Frank after receiving the news of Kleiman's death, 3 March 1959; **23** Letter from Otto Frank to Alice Frank, 8 June 1945; **24** Otto Frank, manuscript, ca. 1968, inv.no. 70; **45, 62** Letter from Victor Kugler to Otto Frank, 11 February 1956.

Other sources:
Citation numbers 30 Declaration of Otto Frank in deposition no. 86, by A.J. van Helden, 1963; National Archive, Central Archive for Extraordinary Proceedings; **51** Interview with Otto Frank in *Welt am Sonntag*, 4 February 1979.

VISUAL CREDITS

The Anne Frank House has made every effort to identify the rightful claimants to the illustrations in this book. If you believe nonetheless that your rights have not been honoured, please contact us.

Explanation: l=left, r=right, t=top, m=middle, b=bottom

©AFF Basel, CH / AFS Amsterdam, NL: front cover (tl, tr, mr, br), p. 2 (4x), p. 16, p. 28, p. 29 (2x), p.30 (t), p. 41, p. 42 (t), p. 47, p. 48, p. 49, p. 50 (2x), p. 52, p. 57, p. 58, p. 59, p. 60 (2x), p. 61, p. 62, p. 110, p. 150 (t).
©AFF / AFS / Photo: Frans Dupont: p. 63.
©AFS: p. 140, p. 141.
©AFS / Frédérik Ruys and Chantal van Wessel: pp. 6-7.

AFS Collection: front cover (tl, mr, bl, br), p. 3 (3x), p. 4 (4x), p. 11, p. 13 (t and b), p. 14, p. 18, p. 21, p. 42 (b), p. 51 (r), p. 70 (2x), p. 71, p. 72, p. 85, p. 86, p. 87, pp. 88-89, p. 90 (b), p. 96 (2x), p. 97 (2x), p. 98, p. 99, p. 100, p. 106, p. 108, p. 115, p. 116, p. 117, p. 118 (2x), p. 123, p. 124, p. 126, p. 127, p. 128, p. 129, p. 130 (2x), p. 135, p. 138, p. 139, p. 147, p. 150 (b), p. 155 (ml, br).
AFS Collection/ ©Bella Kohlweij: p. 51 (l).
AFS Collection/ Ed Fraifeld: p. 37, p. 38.
Anne Frank Archives, ©AFF/AFS: p. 25, p. 26, p. 27, p. 39, p. 40.
Arhiv Republike Slovenije: p. 17.
Gies Collection: front cover (ml), p. 3 (2nd), p. 5, p. 69, p. 79, p. 80 (t), p. 125, p. 136, p. 137, p. 149.
Harry Naeff Pressebilder, Zürich: p. 30 (b).
Lesley Moore: pp. 160-161, pp. 162-163.
©Maria Austria / MAI: back cover (tr), p. 90 (t), p. 105.
©Nederlands Fotomuseum / Bob van Dam: p. 107.
NIOD: p. 13 (m).
Private collection: back cover (ml), p. 15, p. 31, p. 77, p. 78, p. 80 (b), p. 95, p. 155 (mr, bl and bm), p. 156 (2x).
Stadsarchief Amsterdam: p. 148, p. 155 (mr).

COLOPHON

Published and produced by the Anne Frank House

—

Copyright © 2013 Anne Frank House, Amsterdam

Text
Aukje Vergeest
Project management
Anne Frank House
(Chantal d'Aulnis)
Historical research and oversight
Anne Frank House
(Teresien da Silva, Erika Prins)
Visual research
Anne Frank House
(Karolien Stocking Korzen)
Production support
Anne Frank House
(Erica Terpstra)
Editing
Gerti Vos, Ingrid Mersel
Design
Lesley Moore
Typesetting
Strak
(Haiko Oosterbaan)
Printing
Booxs
Illustrated cross section of the Anne Frank House
Vizualism
(Chantal van Wessel, Frédérik Ruys)
Translation
Forest-Flier Editorial Services
(Nancy Forest-Flier)
With thanks to
Gertjan Broek, Menno Metselaar,
Eugenie Martens
(Anne Frank House)

First edition, 2013 (in Dutch, English, German, French, Spanish, Portuguese and Italian)
ISBN/EAN: 978-90-8667-014-7